SECRETS OF A DIGITAL MARKETING NINJA

A Marketer's Guide to Sustainable Growth

By Daniel Rosenfeld

CONTENTS

INTRODUCTION

Every day is a first day for new startups or companies and the last day for others. While there are many reasons for companies to go out of business, failing to reach or influence and retain their market ranks high up on the list. This is often not for lack of trying, but for lack of understanding the basic elements needed to make sustainable growth a reality.

As a Digital Marketer in the high-tech industry, I have had the privilege of working with, and for some of the most innovative companies in the world, both as an employee and as a consultant. I have worked on projects of all sizes, each needing its own strategy and methods to reach its unique target audience and goal.

This book is a collection of my personal experiences, acquired knowledge, and insights, as well as best practices for creating digital marketing strategies to reach your audience and improve your chances of converting them into customers. Throughout the book, I have included many great tips on how to begin your journey to Marketing Ninjahood. These tips have helped me over the years and continue to serve me well.

I started writing this book as a way to refine my own strategies and practices. As the book began to form, I started sharing bits and pieces of it on various online publications such as *Social Media Week*, *Social Media Today*, *TechCrunch*, and other outlets, as a guest blogger.

However, while these posts provided insights into specific topics, they did not give readers a wider picture of how to use the information as part of a strategy. I knew I wanted to create a more comprehensive compilation of all the aspects taken into account when creating an online marketing strategy so that it could be put to use in the real world and help businesses reach their full online potential. I also wanted to help others understand how to modify, distill, or expand their strategy to serve themselves and their customers most efficiently.

Whether you are a marketer, a business owner, or an entrepreneur, increasing your knowledge of digital marketing can serve as a powerful tool for understanding your markets and your customers, including how best to reach and influence them. This is also a great read if you are not in the marketing industry and you seek to understand its intricate inner workings. I have structured the book to help newcomers understand the concepts and make informed decisions with less trial and error, while also providing advanced insights for those who are looking to improve their existing practice.

While there are many digital marketing books, blogs, and vlogs out there which will teach you how to use specific tools or platforms, I will be focusing on the concepts and methodologies for creating a marketing strategy with the goal of real, sustainable growth.

When it comes to companies who are new to online marketing or contemplating investing in an online strategy, there are those who clearly see and understand the value. However, there are those companies who say things like, "We don't believe in online marketing, but are thinking of giving it a shot," or "We want to try online, but we don't want to spend too much money without knowing what our return will be." While the fear is understandable, it is usually either due to past poor experiences with companies that claim to be professional marketers but don't really give the company the time of day, or instances where there was poor communication about the online process. There are also those who think social media is the same as online marketing and don't really understand what it is. Finally, there are those who have honestly never tried any form of online marketing, and their business is mainly focused on cold calling and old-school sales tactics.

The first thing to understand about investing in online marketing is exactly that; it's an investment. It takes time and effort to get it right, but as with most investments it can pay off in the long run.

Here's an example:

A few years ago, a good friend of mine moved to Barcelona, Spain, and opened a vegan restaurant. He started out quite slow, having some customers and slowly building a customer base. But he was not growing fast enough to manage to pay all the bills, and after a few months he turned to me and asked if I could help him grow his customer base with online marketing. I was up for the challenge and we started by reviewing his website and making it more user-friendly. While highlighting the contact options and address, I then asked about his business, what days and hours it was open, and what hours were dead hours.

Armed with this info, I began with simple search campaigns both in English for tourists and in Spanish for locals, using keywords that would match someone looking specifically for a vegetarian or vegan restaurant. Next, we planned a specials deal together which would be offered to people who come to the restaurant during those specific dead hours. I created remarketing campaigns which would target people who visited the restaurant's website only during those hours and showcase the offer.

A few days later, I got a panicked called from my friend. He was worried that the ads were not working and asked that I remove the phone number from the website and replace it with an online booking system. He continued to explain that the phone wouldn't stop ringing and that they were swamped. I burst out laughing. The phone number was only available on the website and the bulk of the visitors to the website, as it was new, were all from the online campaigns.

Once he understood the value of the online campaigns and how they were helping drive his business he would then call me franticly every time his credit card had an issue, worried that the ads might stop serving. His restaurant not only flourished but went on to receive awards.

PART 1:
THE ONLINE MARKETING ECOSYSTEM

Overview

"In the midst of chaos, there is also opportunity."
— Sun Tzu

While the tech media ecosystem is vast and consists of many moving parts, as a whole there is synergy. The base of the ecosystem consists of companies which offer a product or a service. To reach their audience, "Business to Consumer" (B2C) or other companies "Business to Business" (B2B), they require a marketing team, either in-house or outsourced.

It's the online marketer's job to drive branding, create awareness, and generate actions/sales for the company. To achieve this, the marketer has a vast array of tools at their disposal. These range from self-serve advertising platforms such as AdWords, Facebook, and Bing, to business intelligence (BI) tools for competitive analysis such as SimilarWeb, AppAnnie, and BiScience, to analyzing tools which include Google analytics and Mixpanel, to Social tools such as Hootsuite, and the list goes on.

In addition to self-serve platforms, there are also real-time bidding (RTB) marketplaces where marketers and agencies can buy ad space.

This is widely used by hundreds of advertising agencies which buy ad space in bulk and then sell it to marketers with smaller budgets. These agencies also trade ad space among themselves to cater to their respective marketers' needs. Data Management Platforms (DMP's) hold and sort large amounts of user data to enable segmenting and targeting by advertisers. Demand Side Platforms (DSP's) allow advertisers to manage the data and exchanges and utilize real time bidding.

Publishers are the companies that provide the ad space, and they run vast networks of websites containing the ads. Some of the most established companies, such as Google and Facebook, are both publishers and advertising platforms. Google created AdSense, where anyone with a website can sign up to have ads placed on their site and generate income from clicks and impressions. They also created AdWords, where advertisers can pay to put their ads on AdSense active sites known as the Display Network (GDN) as well as on the Google Search Network (GSN). Google then takes a percentage of the ad spend from the advertiser and gives the rest to the site owner.

While this can all be overwhelming at first, a well-established digital marketer's job is to navigate these seas and find the best and cheapest course to reach the company's desired destination. With experience, you learn that the fastest route isn't always the best one to take and that if you plan your voyage well, you may even find treasure along the way, or discover new lands.

Wikipedia defines marketing as, "The activity, set of institutions, and processes for creating, communicating, delivering, and exchanging offerings that have value for customers, clients, partners, and society at large."

I agree with this definition, but there is more to it. Marketing is not only about delivering a message; it's about laying the groundwork for that message to be heard and accepted. It's about shifting perceptions and creating new ones. Marketing not only shapes our future, but it is also embedded in our past.

You might think that marketing is limited to the products you buy, but break it down, and you will see that every decision you think you made on your own was linked to marketing. From where you went to school, to the destinations you visited, your perception of countries, economies, governments, and even the cheaper non-branded clothes you bought were marketed to you as such and influenced your decision.

Many of the largest and most influential companies we admire today are deeply rooted in marketing and advertising. Without marketing they simply would not exist. Google would never have made it without its vast advertising networks which to date generate most of its earnings. Facebook without ads would mean a Facebook in debt for billions, rather than profitable.

Of course, this all started long before Google or Facebook. As consumers, what we see on a daily basis, including ads, commercials, product placements, and billboards, are all the tips of thousands of well-crafted campaigns. These campaigns start long before what the end user will see, think, or do.

Advertising is a commodity similar to real estate, and when you advertise, you essentially buy space. How much space you buy and the location where you buy is what determines both the cost and expected return on your investment (ROI).

All companies share a common goal, regardless of their size or industry; they want to get more money than they spend and thus be profitable. It's that simple. To reach this goal, these companies must formulate a marketing strategy which takes the overall business goals into account. Without a clear goal and a well-rounded strategy in place, most businesses will find themselves on a rollercoaster ride, unsure of how or when it will end.

Master marketers are deemed "Marketing Ninjas" for their superior skills and innate abilities to wield the company strategy, successfully market to their target audience, deliver an impactful message, and exceed the business's expectations. As with any field of study or practice, there are different levels of mastery, knowledge, and specialization. Just like the Ninja, the digital marketer chooses targets wisely, learns their behavior and habits, and predicts their next move. When the Ninja strikes, the target never even realizes that the Ninja was there.

Some marketers prefer to focus on traditional marketing and steer away from online, while others choose to strategize but then do not expand it to hands on experience. Digital marketing stretches throughout many disciplines such as SEM, SEO, ASO, PPC, Social Networks, Content Marketing, Marketing Automation, Email Marketing, Growth Hacking, Mobile Marketing, Building Online Strategies, and much more. In the age of social media and an ever-growing online presence, limiting yourself to traditional marketing limits the reach of your business. It is important to embrace all methods and to understand when and how to use them.

While online and traditional marketing are actually separate methods, in an online world their paths cross often. People nowadays will research products they have seen online before purchasing offline. They review customer feedback while examining the physical product in a store. Some stores will even prompt you to download their app or scan a QR code to get offers. Many people will go to a store to try things on and see what they like, get measurements and make a list to later purchase the same items online at the best price.

Physical stores will ask you for your email so that they can reach out to you with offers. Your email will be used not only to send you mail but also to remarket to you online. Your email may also be used to generate lookalikes of people like you from your social profile. For example, your information may be used by Facebook's algorithm to find more people with similar interests, age groups, geographic location, and habits in order to allow the store to extend their marketing reach to a wider target audience likely to be interested in their products.

Traditional and online marketing are becoming more intertwined, and with the marketer's understanding that when correctly used to complement each other, sales and customer satisfaction increase. Companies like Facebook now offer offline tracking for online campaigns, so that marketers can see the effect their online marketing has in the real world.

The more knowledge and experience you gain from each discipline, the more tools you acquire, the broader your understanding, and the greater your chances of successfully leveraging your marketing ecosystem.

Digital What?

In the marketing sector, there are many titles and positions such as PPC managers, SEM, or SEO managers. The bigger and more complicated the marketing becomes, the more people with specialized skills need to be added to the team. However, the two main titles people refer to when describing a well-rounded, multi-disciplined internet based marketing position are Online Marketers and Digital Marketers.

Both online and digital marketers are highly skilled web marketers with knowledge of your campaign's marketing landscape. Digital marketers take it a step further and include mobile, tablet, and video marketing rather than focusing exclusively on web marketing. The terms can be used interchangeably as the industry has turned to one of a mobile first outlook. This means that all online marketers focus on mobile as well; thus the only real difference is simply the title chosen.

Traditional marketing (pre-digital marketing), relied mainly on newspapers, pamphlets, brochures, billboards, and posters in order to reach audiences. Later, radio and television brought significant changes to the marketing industry by providing advertisers more ways to reach a broad, tuned-in audience.

The internet has not only increased the volume of our audience; the real revolution is in the ability to target people globally, individually, and immediately. If you know who you want to target, what it is you want those people to do, and how to quantify success, then there *is* a way for you to effectively do it online.

One thought was stuck in the back of my mind when I was in my Digital Marketing Ninja diapers: The importance of exploring and reading everything I could about online marketing, watching endless YouTube videos, reading blog posts, joining newsletters, RSS feeds, Podcasts, books—you name it.

Marketing has been around for ages, but the basics are simple: You have something you want to sell, you want to reach as many people as you can to influence them to buy your product or service.

It was clear to me that the evolution of technology provided newer, broader, and simpler ways to reach your audience. What wasn't clear was why marketing techniques keep changing. What I mean is, why wouldn't a commercial from the 1960's work today?

Every month I hear about new methods and tactics. You can clearly see it on TV and online ads. The tactics and terminologies keep changing, but the goal remains the same. Thousands of media companies are formed every year, each trying to get a piece of the action and offering new technologies for serving ads, monetization, and analyzing.

But humans have remained the same physically: we all still have two arms, two legs, and one head. Is all this progress and constant changing of marketing methods really necessary?

While physically we may seem unchanged, people are always evolving on the psychological, cultural, and social levels. We are not just doing everything faster; we are getting more and more tech reliant. At the age when I was learning to ride a bicycle, our children are learning how to program and use computers, phones, drones, and new technologies.

Once, people aspired to become lawyers or doctors. Now we want to be entrepreneurs, programmers, and engineers. We are getting more sophisticated, and marketing is not only trying to keep up with the pace—it's also helping to shape it.

Behind every successful product, there are successful marketers. Every product that influences our world impacts our progress.

Marketers look for trends—things they can use to relate to audiences and then shift their strategies to meet them. They not only create the trends, but they must also keep up and adapt to them.

The Role of a Digital Marketer

With the Internet literally in every person's pocket, on our wrists, and soon our heads, people are spending more than nine hours a day on average online. Thus it is no surprise that digital marketing has become a primary focus for many companies. It has become the main marketing technique many choose to use to reach their target audience due to the highly targeted, trackable and scalable methods digital offers. Therefore, a digitally savvy individual is needed to take charge and lead the digital marketing assault for your company.

The digital marketer is responsible for generating strategies, gathering assets, building the campaign funnels, overseeing execution, optimization, and ensuring the company sees positive ROI. As the digital ecosystem grows daily and markets shift, the digital marketer must also be constantly attuned to these changes and adapt to these shifts.

While some might see the role of the marketer as solely responsible for marketing efforts, more often than not, a digital marketer will be highly involved in product and sales decisions which can affect the marketing efforts, and will also delve into the technical aspects as these too can affect overall success.

Any marketer knows it's one thing to get people through the door, it's another to close the sale. Marketing, product, sales, and tech departments need to work in tandem to give the user/customer a holistic and user-friendly experience. Everything from onboarding to the colors and images chosen for both the product and marketing materials and site performance needs to be seamless.

Another example of this is with features. Often a product team will focus on features they believe will improve the user experience. This may be great for engagement and retention, but the focus may be lost on features aimed at growth. A product which does not promote organic growth will have to spend many more resources trying to extend its reach.

For a feature to promote growth, it would either have to promote sharing, inviting, or word of mouth which would lead existing users to promote your product to their friends. Or the feature would have to be news or PR worthy, in which case blogs and online publications would write about it, and it would increase exposure for the product.

The best way to fuel this kind of thinking is to collaborate with product managers and create a chart/table of current and planned features. The marketer needs to conduct a competitor's analysis and research user interaction in order to understand the value each feature brings, and how certain features will influence customer interactions and sales.

The marketer should also work collaboratively with the internal product team to understand similar features. It's helpful to gather other data points such as percent of feature use and how customers who used the feature were affected by it. This information will help the team understand what value your current features bring and where to focus future feature development.

Collecting this type of necessary customer feedback can only help the team. For example, there could be an unfortunate situation where many months were spent developing certain features or product aspects, which, in practice, did not deliver the desired result. If the correct research would have been conducted, better features would have been created, thus generating the desired result and not wasting time and money developing a less than desirable feature.

Take, for example, a vehicle. The product designer might have a great idea and want to create extra room for cup holders, special seat adjustment buttons, and an air-conditioning vent from the car's roof. All these might very well be valid features, but the marketer after doing their research know that people are more interested in a new in-car entertainment system. So while the new cup holders and air-conditioning may sound great, they likely won't help sell the car, while focusing on a great entertainment system would help the sales and marketing team sell more.

It has become an unanticipated job of a successful marketer to educate the company about the importance of involving the marketer in all aspects of development and sales of the service or product. The marketer has a role to play in the earliest stage of development. The marketer's early input may be crucial to avoid costly mistakes later in the product. It's critical to involve the marketer early on to guide the development towards the later growth of the product, and not just its functionality. Each person who proposes an input to the product views the end product according to their ideals of aesthetics and technical features.

In this instance, the role of the marketer is to objectively view the product or service as an observer who bases their input on market research, competitor analysis, and market trends. In this light, they would determine which aspects will sell and which will be irrelevant or even hinder growth and sales.

Managing Expectations

A common issue digital marketers face is being asked for sales forecasts, or what budget will be needed in order to achieve the objective. While these are, without a doubt, great questions and ones that need to be answered, they are questions you should not attempt to guess the answers to, but instead, the answers should be the result of serious and strategic consideration. You might be tempted to make an educated guess based on experience from previous projects. But, this is probably not a good idea, as each project needs to be evaluated on its own. There is not a one-size-fits-all for every project.

Understandably the customer will want to see a complete strategy before they commit. However, it is not always possible to complete a full strategy at the beginning stages of a project, as benchmarks are needed to evaluate and decide on the best and most profitable course to take. Sometimes you can only provide an estimate by conducting as much research and planning as possible to help manage future expectations. Additionally, explaining the online process, such as learning and optimization, and benchmarking a time frame for these stages will help avoid situations where it may seem that the strategy is under delivering, while in reality, the gradual growth is simply part of the process.

In other words, while your client wants to understand what they will get from the online marketing efforts, it's important to educate them about the online process and the various stages needed to reach their goals. By doing so, they will be more understanding should more time be needed to reach a positive ROI and will give you the space and resources needed to get the job done.

Process Management

Process Management is looking at a process or flow and understanding the big picture, then making sure all the elements are aligned correctly to support and reach the goal. While process management is generally associated with human resources and looking at an organization's processes, the idea behind it can be carried into the marketing department. Most marketing departments are so busy multitasking that it's easy to lose track of the big picture, focusing only on the current marketing goals.

Many times, this leads to shifts in focus and eventually results in achieving short-term milestones, which don't necessarily bring the company closer to its actual long-term objectives. It is also important to remember that marketing is part of a process that is usually accompanied by the product department, sales, and tech departments. If all of these elements are not synchronized, the whole strategy can experience turmoil. Communication between departments, cross channel planning, and synergy are key to long-term success.

Imagine the following scenario: You have a great idea of how to get 20,000 daily visitors to your site and triple sales overnight by signing on an influencer with a huge relevant audience. You plan out your strategy, change all the website copy and ads to fit with the influencer's messaging, and then it happens, the first post goes out. You are looking at your real-time analytics dashboard, and you witness a huge surge of visitors—-sales start exploding. Great job!

An hour later you get a call from the sales director asking what happened, why are they getting so many calls? It turns out they are low on staff today and can't handle the load. Suddenly, you get another call from the server team. The website has crashed from the overload. The servers were not equipped to manage the traffic load. This might sound a bit far-fetched, but it happens all the time. Yes, I'll say it, even though we've all heard it before: Communication is key. Good communication is important not only within your department but for all parties affected by your actions.

With marketing, the ecosystem changes so fast that many marketers try to keep up with everything, rather than keeping their focus on what they originally planned. For example, the goal of a quarter could be to build awareness and open the market in Los Angeles. The whole team starts researching LA and looking for opportunities, building strategies, reaching out to vendors, creating marketing materials, and everything needed to reach that goal. One morning, three weeks into this process, an article comes out about a new type of ad format that Facebook is launching that will only be available at first for targeting Texas. Poor process management would lead many marketers to abandon the fully processed LA plan and shift towards Texas. Or worse, Texas would now be added and all focus, time, and budget would now be split up. Imagine if this happened once a week or even on a daily basis.

The main takeaway for effective process management is not to simply ignore your surroundings, but to understand them. When you encounter new options, step back, evaluate your original plan, and consider whether this new information or tool could help you achieve that goal. Ask yourself, how much of a distraction will it be, and do you really have to jump on this marketing wagon right away or can it wait?

It is important to keep in mind that marketing is constantly in motion. To achieve your goals, you need to do more than just keep trying out the latest and greatest. Instead, you need to use your experience to create a game plan, get the whole company behind it, and then follow it through. There is a middle-ground between rigidity and flexibility, as you should not be deterred from your original goal or plan, but should be able to spot genuine opportunities to further the product or service.

Partnerships: Leveraging Your Network

There is just so much a person can accomplish alone. You can be the best digital marketer on the planet, but for a business to reach its full potential, it takes more. The word partnership once meant a situation where both parties provided each other with equal value. In today's business world, however, it is widely used to suggest a situation where you pay for a service as a suggestion that what you get for your money is more than just a service. Companies don't want to position themselves as only service providers, but rather as entities that are more invested in your company's success—a partner.

There are many types of partnerships you can leverage from media companies who may have broader targeting options, to actual partnerships where you truly do simply help each other. It can be as simple as trading ads on a website. For example, both companies place the other company's ads on their website, thus increasing the exposure for both. Creating cross promotions can even be as simple as blog mentions, linking, etc.

Networking is not only recommended, but it's also crucial to your success. You never know what may come out of a simple LinkedIn introduction or a five-minute call. Some people feel harassed when approached by vendors asking to partner, but giving that spammy looking email a look over may sometimes be exactly what you need or are looking for.

Another type of partnership, which is invaluable, is with support managers and account managers. Most respectable companies have support managers and account managers, usually to help on bigger accounts. When I started out with AdWords, for example, I spent an hour each day on the phone with their support, asking everything I could think of to get to know the system better. Sure, there are articles and blogs, but the technical support provides more than just technical help, they provide insight and suggestions. Once I progressed, I moved to an account manager, which was invaluable, not only for the deep analysis and suggestions provided but also for the guidance and assurance in decisions. Sure, you can go at it alone, but you will learn much more and progress faster both personally and professionally when you build and foster the right partnerships.

PART 2:
CRAFTING YOUR MARKETING STRATEGY

Overview

> "If opportunity doesn't knock, build a door."
> —Milton Berle

When it comes to online marketing, strategy is key. You can have all the skills and knowledge, but without truly understanding your goals, your market, and even your own organization or the one you're working for, you will most likely fail. It may seem obvious, but it's worth repeating, that while the ultimate goal of marketing may be sales, there are a large number of intermediate goals towards which the marketer should strive. Intermediate goals may include subscriptions, lead generation, social interactions and company branding.

So how do you go about formulating an online strategy? It all starts with identifying your goals, and understanding whether or not the goals are well-formulated and realistic. Goals should then be broken down into smaller and manageable subgoals. For example, a main goal could be the generating of sales, and a subgoal could be growing a social presence. Next, quantify the goals; for example, X sales and Y followers within Z amount of time, i.e., 50 sales and 200 followers within one month.

Once the goals are defined, your next step is to determine the financial resources allocated to achieving these goals. This is not yet your budget, but your target cost per acquisition. In other words, how much you can afford to pay to acquire a new customer?

For example, let's say you sell a garden bench and the sales price is $100. You must first determine how much of the $100 remains as profit after the production costs or cost of goods (COGs). Once you know that number, you will have the high limit for acquisition. This is the amount you can spend for one sale, which will result in breaking even, or zero earnings and zero loss. You learn it will cost $40 to produce each bench; therefore, there is a $60 margin for marketing. Any sale acquisition which is below $60 is deemed profitable; any sale made at $60 breaks even, and any sale above $60 is ineffective, as the product is sold at a loss.

Naturally, profitability is not only in the cost per single sale, but also has to do with scale.

You need to understand how many units need to be sold, and at what cost per acquisition (CPA) in order for the strategy to be deemed a success.

Of course, the overall budget is also important, but at this stage, you don't yet have enough information about the target audiences, platforms, and reach needed to make that assessment. Therefore, the focus of the idea is to work from your goals and then find the budget to meet those goals. This will help you better allocate your budget and keep your strategy focused.

Let's say a marketer is asked how much funding is needed to sell 500 units. To give a realistic estimate, you must understand the cost of acquisition, which platforms will be used, the percentage of the target audience available on each platform, and the cost of advertising on each selected platform.

It is important to understand that while this research is crucial for building your strategy, you will only really know actual costs and CPA once you go live with your campaigns, as these costs are based on real people clicking and converting. Your Target CPA is therefore exactly that, a target, and the strategy will aim to reach that target. The strategy is meant to guide you and give you the best chance to succeed. How well the strategy is implemented, the landing pages, the messaging, and the audience themselves will determine the final outcome.

While you may have an amazing strategy in hand, getting results takes time, for this reason, you must also add a learning period to your plan. You are running ads, but you still don't know how effective the results will be. Even though this period may not yield any profit, it is a crucial stage of the process.

When you invest in digital marketing, you don't only buy ads; you also buy information. You learn what works and what doesn't work. That information includes which text ads or display ads appeal more to your audience, which placements they prefer, which keywords work best and insights on your target audience provided by the platform used. This is valuable information which takes time to acquire, but this information is just as valuable if not more so than actual sales since the information acquired during this period will help fuel your marketing efforts in the long term.

The marketer's efforts may not immediately produce sales or signups, and this needs to be explained before the launching of the campaigns, as many expect profitability straight away. After this period, the marketer gets to use all the gathered information to optimize the campaigns, thus working towards the acquisition goal.

Once you have an idea of what your goals are, make sure to set benchmarks by drawing clear outlines and borders for what success or failure will look like. Your strategy should not only include your goals but also have a scale of success.

For example, you may be expected to sell a unit for no more than $30, and you have been asked to sell 1,000 units. That part may be clear, but you also need to understand over what period of time you are required to sell 1,000 units. Also, are there instances where it is okay to exceed $30? And if so, then by how much? Selling 1,000 units may be the company's goal, but if you sell 860 units would that be considered a failure?

Having these benchmarks set makes your expectations clear, which is important to keep the company happy. If you are working for a company, they will see that even if you did not achieve the end goal, you still managed to reach some of the benchmark expectations. Meeting these benchmarks will help the company feel more comfortable with your efforts. If you are building the strategy for your own business, these benchmarks will help you monitor and improve your own efforts.

Research is one of the most important aspects of a digital marketing strategy. There are many levels of research you should conduct before starting a project. Some of these are less obvious than others.

Start by researching your own client or your own business, not only what they do and what their goals are, but also what their expectations are. Does the client or company have a clear vision of what they expect to achieve, and is it a reasonable one? Is it something you are equipped for or do you perhaps need to bring in additional professionals for assistance, such as graphic designers, content creators, social media managers, media buyers, etc.?

Next, don't just briefly research the company or client, but really investigate them. Look for articles written about them which could shed light on how potential and existing clients perceive the company. Ask what the current issues are and where they need to improve. Make no mistake; every company has its issues. Look at their digital assets. Are they set up correctly? For example, do their assets correlate with their messaging? If it's an online business with a store, how is the store set up and does it work? Look at their social media accounts. Are they putting enough effort into social? Are they on the correct social channels? What does the social conversation look like, what are customers saying? Investigate the buyer's journey. Would you buy on their site?

Many people research a product before placing an order. Do the same. Try and come at it from an unbiased perspective. Would you truly want the product you are promoting or would you have gone in another direction, and if so why? Answering these questions will help you understand the strengths and weaknesses of the product or company. This will help you plan a strategy taking both into account.

The job of a Digital Marketer is not only to set up campaigns but to make sure they do everything in their power and knowledge to reach the goal they have been tasked with. Sometimes this means not taking a job, especially if the marketer doesn't believe in the way the client is proceeding and the latter are unwilling to apply the marketer's advice. The marketer may be better holding off until the clients make the necessary changes and improve their assets as required.

Once the marketer has researched the company, has a full understanding of the task, and has decided to undertake the challenge, then they can move on to researching the industry they are in. This can be done by conducting competitive analysis, finding target audiences, and choosing the best platforms for the job.

At the end of the day, it's the digital marketer's responsibility and reputation that is at stake, so they should only take on a project they have full confidence in, both from their own abilities and that of the company.

My Pillars of Online Marketing

There are those who would say there is a science to marketing strategies. I think it's less science and more mathematics. If you have your basics down and know how to use them, reaching the correct solution is likely. I base my strategies and campaigns on six fundamental pillars:

- Relevance
- Mindset
- Messaging
- Buying Cycle
- Engagement
- Retention

Understanding these concepts and learning how to integrate them into every strategy you build will significantly increase your likelihood of success.

Relevance

How do most digital marketers rate their success at reaching their target audience? They look for hard data on click-throughs, length of time spent on the page, even the number of likes and shares a piece of content has on social media. These metrics all amount to one major thing (I assume you don't need a drum roll here), yes, it's relevance.

You can pay as much as you want for clicks, but if you're offering content which isn't relevant to your target audience, you will have poor performing metrics. Sure, some people will click, but they will most likely not perform your desired action. So if you are thinking of literally "selling ice to Eskimos" you should probably reconsider doing it via a pay per click (PPC) channel.

On AdWords, Google's advertising platform, ads are rated with a "Quality Score." The algorithm behind the concept looks at the keywords within text ads and matches them to the keywords chosen in that campaign's ads, as well as the ad's landing page the ads send to. The higher the compatibility between all three elements, the greater the relevance score.

Additionally, they look at your bid and the Click Through Rate (CTR), which shows how relevant the ads really are to users. All of these comprise the "Quality Score." As a result, ads with a higher quality score than competing ads can win bids, even if the monetary bid is lower. For example: let's say I bid $3 and a competitor bids $4. My ad has a Quality Score of seven, while they have a Quality Score of five. My ads might show before theirs, and I will still pay the lower bid I set.

Why would Google care more about relevance than bids? Well, it comes down to a few factors. First of all, it gives searchers a better experience to find things they are looking for. Secondly, it makes financial sense. Google understands that more relevant ads receive more clicks, so they prefer to get ten clicks on a relevant ad for a bid of $2, then three clicks for $3. This is not just a feature on AdWords, it's the base of the whole platform and is one of the most important aspects of running well converting and low-cost AdWords

Campaigns. In addition, it is an understanding you can take with you to any platform.

While not all platforms take into account the same exact parameters, they usually have some kind of relevance score based on CTR. Preparing your assets based on relevance will help ensure your audience has a good experience. This, in turn, will improve your chances of conversions and will ensure you are using your budget wisely by limiting unwanted, irrelevant clicks.

Mindset

Social networks serve a purpose. They entertain us, teach us, allow us to interact with each other, and even help us find our spouses. Marketing via social networks is an important part of an overall marketing strategy.

When referring to Social Media, most people understand it as online platforms, which allow people to interact with each other from the comfort of their work, home, or phone. Social Media has made it easier to interact with strangers while keeping tabs on friends and family. Every month, more and more social channels are launched, all wanting to be the next Facebook or Twitter.

Facebook came out as a very broad medium, which in turn opened the market for tailored niche media such as LinkedIn. The game, at the moment, is looking for new and exciting ways to interact and use social media. Twitter lets you be social in a very minimalist way; Reddit lets readers decide what's worth sharing; and so on.

These networks all play on our simple human need to interact with each other by understanding how we interact and what interests us. Social networks rely heavily on advertising for income. This opens new opportunities for advertisers but also introduces fierce competition over budgets. This competition led Facebook to release graph search to compete with Google and add targeting by title to compete with LinkedIn; they have recently opened Facebook Workplace which will no doubt expand their B2B targeting capabilities.

The bigger the competition, the stronger these platforms will fight to hold on to their users.

If they can't compete, they will try to buy each other out. Advertisers can reach their target audience on a variety of platforms. You can probably reach similar if not the same audiences on Twitter, Facebook, LinkedIn, and YouTube.

So how do you choose where to place your budget? You could base your decision on costs per action, reach, or even a flip of a coin—but that might not get you the results you are looking for. There is one common oversight when it comes to choosing a platform, and that is mindset and intent. One of the most important questions marketers have to ask themselves before any campaign (on any platform) is not where the audience is, but *why* they are there.

Depending on your target audience, the reasons they are interacting on a certain platform can vary. For example, Pinterest is an aspirational platform, Facebook has a broad audience but is known for a place to connect with friends and family, LinkedIn targets professionals, and Twitter appeals to their audience as a global messaging board letting people get snapshots of topics and individuals they care about and to whom they express themselves. All of these platforms are open to a variety of users, all different ages, with various careers, interests, and cultures, yet, they appeal due to a particular method of usability that speaks to their users.

Therefore when selecting a platform for your strategy, it is important to ask yourself, "Is the type of content I am creating matching up with the platform I am planning to use?" You also need to understand what each platform provides, and if your target audience would be interested in your content if it were presented to them on that platform. If not, perhaps it belongs elsewhere. On Facebook, people like to catch up on friends, activities, and things they liked. They tend to prefer real images of people and not well-edited ads.

The vibe on Facebook is fun and social, so it would make more sense to market products that match that feeling. On LinkedIn, people are either looking for their next job or networking on a professional level, in which case it would make sense to advertise products or services related to a professional network.

This is true not only to social media but to any placement you select to target. If you want to place ads on websites, it's not enough to find websites that have to do with the industry you are targeting; you also need to understand what people visiting that site are looking for.

Here's an example: Your product is extreme sports travel insurance, and your research shows that people who are single are 80 percent more likely to be active in extreme sports. You already target all the extreme sports related websites, and you are looking to expand your reach. One thought that comes to mind is dating sites, as most people on dating sites are single, making the likelihood of a percentage of those users to be extreme sports travelers. Should you place your ads on dating sites?

Well, the first rule I go by is to try anything. You never know what you might not have factored in. That said, people on dating sites are there with a very specific purpose. Ads that may distract from that purpose are less likely to be clicked on, as the mindset on a dating site is very clear. Your ad, in this case, would have to make sense for that mindset. While your audience may be on the site, they are most probably not in the mindset for extreme sports but rather looking for a mate. Targeting your audience on extreme travel websites and blogs as well as extreme sports fashion sites will probably work better in this case. This doesn't mean you can't also find a combination that works, for example, if you were to target sites that offer extreme sports trips for singles, you would probably do very well.

If you understand why someone visits a certain platform, you can understand where to target them and how to approach them. Next time you are trying to figure out where to place your ads, ask yourself where they would be most appreciated, and if your audience will have the right mindset to receive them. Alternatively, if you are set on reaching an audience on a platform that does not hold the correct mindset for your product, try to match your messaging or offer to the correct mindset.

Messaging

When you are marketing to your audience, whether be it with text, image, or video, you have to say something. When it comes to the performance of a campaign you could have everything right, but get your messaging wrong, and it could spell disaster. Messaging should be compelling, easy to read or comprehend, and straightforward. Potential customers should be able to understand what you offer, how it could benefit them, and what you would like them to do—all with a single glance. While most attribute messaging to text, all aspects of your marketing contribute to the messaging. As the saying goes, "A picture is worth a thousand words."

Messaging should rely heavily on the type of marketing you wish to achieve. If your goal is awareness and market penetration, you could use vague messaging to create mystery and try to get as many people as possible to click on your ad, reach your landing page (LP), and learn of the existence of your service or product.

However, if your goal is to increase sales, having vague messaging could end up costing you dearly, especially if you are running pay per click campaigns (PPC). Nothing is worse than having thousands of clicks by people who are not your target audience and who are not converting.

You might then suggest using a different method, like cost per million (CPM), which isn't based on paying for clicks, but rather for how many people view the ads. That, however, is just perception as the result you look for in CPM is achieving a cheaper CPC. While CPM might produce a slightly cheaper CPC, the results may be the same.

Vague and mysterious messaging may lead to a higher click rate (CTR), but of a poor-quality audience, you will most probably end up spending the same or even more to get users who do not convert. Therefore, you need to decide what your goal is and create content to match that goal with your target audience in mind.

If your messaging is too specific, then you might lose those potential customers that do not necessarily fit within the parameters of your target audience. Well-formulated messaging entices the viewer and provides them with the information or action needed in as short a time as possible, similar to an elevator pitch where the objective is to be able to get a meeting or client on board within a short elevator ride.

Buying Cycle

Every person goes through a buying cycle, whether we realize it or not. Buying cycles can be shortened when it's a product or service we know or must have. The basic stages of the buying cycle are awareness, research, evaluation, competitor analysis, and decision. For some products, the process could take minutes, while for others (such as a mortgage, or that super-cool drone, or pair of heels you *really* want but are slightly out of your budget) it can take weeks and even months.

Awareness is the first stage. It can come directly from the product through advertising; it can come from PR, or through word of mouth. This stage is critical because it is where the potential customer gets their first impression. Think of it as an extra reminder to why providing a good user experience, customer service, and a positive social presence is so important. Many new customers will get their first impression based on what they are told by your former and current customers. Think of every interaction with your potential and current customers as a first impression to maximize your customer's awareness in a positive way.

During the **research** stage, potential customers dig deeper in your product or service. They may review your website, look at social networks, read or watch reviews, ask friends, or ask on forums for recommendations. Therefore, it is important that your website be an effective resource. They should be able to find what they need quickly. It should be well-organized and provide an easy to understand explanation of your product or service and how it works. Your interactions on social media should make your audience feel as if you are an expert in your field or industry.

The research phase can help your potential customer build trust in your product or service, but it could also make them want to run to a competitor. You cannot avoid bad reviews, but you should try to answer them to the best of your ability, moving the conversation to a private message when possible. Show your potential customers that you will respond to their concerns. This is another way to build their trust in you and your brand.

Once all the data they believe they need has been collected, the customer will reach the **evaluation** stage. Many times this stage has less to do with the product or service, and more to do with inner conflicts: Can I afford this? Do I really need it? Should I wait until the next version comes out? The more compelling the marketing, the greater the chances of a potential customer completing this phase with a favorable outcome.

You might be asking yourself why I have placed **competitive analysis** as a separate entity from research. This stage has a lot to do with the personality of the customer and the need your messaging leaves with them. Is your offer giving a sense of urgency? Does it really seem to customers like a great deal? Depending on such factors, your customers might not even bother to check what else is on the market.

Finally, after your potential customer has gone through at least some of these phases, they are ready to make a **decision**. The key is knowing how to reach your prospects with the right message at the right stage of their buying cycle to either convert them on the spot or to provide them with enough input to move them to the next stage.

Engagement

Many companies will spare no expense in acquiring new customers with vast advertising campaigns and offers but neglect those customers soon after. Unless your product or service is a one-time offer, engagement can be the difference between a happy, return customer and one you will never see again. An engaged customer is not only more likely to return and purchase additional products from you but is also more likely to become a brand ambassador and drive other purchasers your way.

Engagement does not always have to come after a product purchase—it can also be part of it. For example, there are many airlines offering low-cost travel. Which one will you remember, the flight where you were treated like a low-cost passenger or the flight where the flight attendant smiled at you, engaged with you, and offered you good service? Sometimes the price doesn't even matter; it's the small things that leave an impression on you.

I have owned many cars during my life. With every single car I purchased, once I had the keys in my hand, I never heard from them again unless they were trying to sell me something. Three years ago, I purchased the most basic model of a Mini Cooper. A week after I left the lot with my new car, I received a phone call from Mini asking if everything was fine with the car. A few months later, I was invited to a free concert for Mini owners. Just a few months after that, I received a letter offering a free checkup before winter. Over and over again, they have reached out to me and engaged me. I have not only become an owner but an ambassador, telling all my friends it's the best purchase I have ever made. They turned a simple car into much more than that.

The next time I purchase a car, it will most likely be a Mini, not because it's necessarily a better car from others in its price range, in fact, I could probably get a better financial deal, but because it has become much more than a car—it's a service. They made me feel like someone cares. They went out of their way to engage me and have shown me value that a price tag simply can't replace.

Acquisition is not the end of a customer's buying cycle; it's the beginning of an ongoing relationship. If your marketing strategy is built around acquiring customers or users but lacks an engagement plan, you will find yourself constantly fighting to keep up with the churn rather than keeping up with new and returning customers. With quality engagement, you can avoid the costs of constantly competing for those new customers, but instead, reinvest in those customers you already have.

Retention

While some may claim that engagement and retention are the same, in reality, engagement is only part of the retention scheme. Engagement can help support retention, because the more engaged your audience is, the more likely they are to stick around. However, real retention comes from having a great product and making sure your customers understand its full potential, and how to use it.

The more the product is used, the more it becomes part of your life, and the less likely you are to give it up. A few years ago, Starbucks changed their logo slightly by removing a few elements in an attempt to clean it up and give it a fresh look. They were soon bombarded with hate mail, angry social media posts, and outraged customers. Many people could not understand these reactions.

Why would anyone care about the design of the Starbucks cup? For the angry customers, Starbucks is not merely a cup of coffee; it is a significant part of their day and life, and it's embedded into their consciousness. When Starbucks makes a change, it affects them on a personal level. When customers complain about redundant elements of a business, that business has truly reached a high level of retention.

When it comes to retention, there is more to it than just the online component. Naturally, the quality of the product, the customer service, and other elements are out of the digital marketer's hands. For this reason, a big part of optimization is collaboration. By taking part in customer support, hearing the issues, the concerns, and complaints customers have, you can work together to improve customer expectations and even sales.

Additionally, you can use this inner networking to make suggestions and help the sales funnel. For example, having a coupon added to a physical product which can be redeemed on the website for a future sale can help bring a customer back. Giving customers more than they asked for can get you more than you expect to get.

How to Tackle Competitive Analysis

Part of any marketing strategy is competitive analysis. When it comes to competitor analysis, the objective is to research your competitors, understand how they operate, and determine what tools, strategies, and methods they use. To get off on the right foot, you need to define what the analysis is for. Are you aiming to beat your competition, learn from them, or maybe even partner with them? To be successful, however, takes more than research and good BI tools. Sometimes competitive analysis can get you more than you are bargaining for.

Many companies look at others in their space and right away label them competition, but that's not always the case. For example, a high-end burger joint may consider the neighboring McDonald's competition. Sure, they both sell burgers, but the consumer who goes to a burger joint selling $10 burgers is probably not the same customer buying a Big Mac for $1. It would be similar to a Porsche dealership considering a Toyota dealership as competition. If they considered McDonald's competition, they would have to start lowering prices to the point they would be losing money since McDonald's wins by bulk buying and owning their own farms and factories.

Before you start analyzing competitors, establish who your competitors actually are. Additionally, ask yourself if there are companies that are not competitors, but are companies you can learn from. While competitor analysis is aimed at your competition, you may want to expand your research and look for companies who share your audience, but do not compete with you directly. They could teach you just as much as any competitor and have the potential for partnership. As an example, take two airlines, both have a fleet of planes and work hard to secure customers. However, none of their destinations cross paths. They are both in the extremely competitive airline business but are not direct competitors. This would open up various opportunities to leverage each company's offerings and audience to support and expand each other's business, a simple example being each promoting the other's destinations.

Too many times I have witnessed companies getting over excited when they find a piece of information about their competitor's operation. And while sometimes that enthusiasm may be valid, you should not put all your trust in your competitor and blindly copy them. Just because they are a competitor doesn't mean they are doing everything right. It's easy to look at the top company in your industry and simply try to copy everything they do.

Many companies try to be the next Google or Facebook, but what worked for them might not work as well for you. It's great to learn from successful companies, but you have to keep in mind they have the infrastructure, budget, and experience to do what they are doing. Moreover, the bigger a company gets, the more mistakes they are likely making.

Google, for example, has more failed products (Google Buzz, Google Notebook) than winning ones; it's just that the wins make up for the losses. Imagine if you were a startup and decided to emulate one of those Google products. One failure for an early stage startup could be too big a loss to recover from.

Make sure you understand what you are analyzing. Companies use many tools for various reasons. It's not enough to know what tools they are using and how, you need to understand why. A tool such as the Chrome extension "Tag Explorer" can tell you what tags are on a competitor's site. For example, if they have a tag by Facebook, Google, Mixpanel and so on, it can give some insight into what tools they are using, but many of these tools can be used for various products offered by each platform. It's important to gain an understanding of how they might be used before jumping to conclusions.

You also need to know your place in the market. Your competitor might be doing things your company simply isn't ready for. Emulating them at the wrong time in your company's state could end up being very pricey. Don't go all in on an idea just because it's working for someone else; they might have other reasons or elements in place for their success. If possible, try to find out what they were doing when their company was in a stage similar to yours.

See the big picture. Most successful companies have a method to their madness. It's not one thing they do; it's a collective effort. They have various levels of support. Before you choose to go down their path, you need to make sure you have the same support structure set up. Above all, it's important to believe in yourself. It's great to see what the competition is doing, but too many times that leads companies away from what they originally set out to do. If your company is failing, and the competitor analysis is an attempt to steer the ship, that's fine.

But if all is going well and your own strategy is working, don't steer away too much or you might be headed for an iceberg.

Competitive analysis can be a great way for a company to learn its ecosystem, define goals, and even perfect strategies, as long as you keep in mind that the grass isn't always greener on the other side. Sometimes when you see a flower, you encounter a thorn bush.

PART 3:

FINDING YOUR MARKET

Overview

The term, target audience is used to describe the specific audience an advertiser wishes to target for their product or service. One of the biggest mistakes made both by marketers and companies is that they approach the task of finding target audiences from a personal perspective.

When it comes to target audiences, don't try to answer the question, "Why would I use this product?" Instead, ask "who" would use it and "how?"

Most products, even the ones you would least expect, have an audience, and that audience may not think, look or act like you. While a target audience can be created using a combination of attributes such as age, nationality, religion, location, interests, etc., it is important, to begin with a finer distinction of the group you want to focus on.

First, determine what kind of audience you want to target based on what you want to achieve. Are you seeking a Business to Business (B2B) or Business to Consumer (B2C) connection? Both types of audiences act very differently because they have different considerations when making the purchase. An individual making a purchase defines their own will and needs and looks at their budget and how the purchase may affect them, then weighs the pros and cons.

A professional who is purchasing on behalf of their company will, like the individual, explore the company's needs and budget before making a decision regarding a service or product. While they will not be impacted personally as a result of the order, their reputation and possibly job may be on the line. As the best interests of the company must be taken into account regarding budget and quality, B2B software selection, for example, can have a vast impact on the company. Choosing the wrong CRM or advertising partner can cost the company thousands and sometimes millions. For this reason, B2B customers tend to do a lot more research than your average personal buyer, and your marketing materials will generally have to provide in-depth information.

Are you targeting potential users for your app or buyers for your product or service? The type of business you are marketing will also influence how and where you seek out your customers. Are you looking to target your audience directly or indirectly? For example, you can target potential customers, or you can target influencers of that market and media professionals. With B2B, for example, do you want to target company employees or only executives? You may want to target multiple segments as part of your overall strategy, but understanding who those audiences are is the first step. Once you have an idea of your target audience, split them into three broad categories:

> **Presumed audience:** is based on the internal research and analysis you have conducted to understand who is currently using your product. It's important to know who is already using your product or service because this will allow you to target a similar audience.

> **Assumed audience:** is comprised of who you believe *should* be using your product or service. For example, if the product you are marketing is a vacuum cleaner, you could assume that your target audience would be located in areas or countries that are known to be dusty, or where it's customary or trendy for people to use carpeting. You could also have a preconception that your audience is mainly housewives.

Discoverable audience: is pretty much everyone else since you never know how or why people may choose to use your product. Keeping an open mind about your target audience can sometimes yield unexpected results.

One question I am always asked is, "If you know who is using the service or product, why bother with assumptions and discovery?" The answer is rooted in the human traits that make most companies fail: prejudice and comfort.

When a company first launches a product, their tendency is to target what they already know and assume to be their best customer. By doing this, companies often start with the assumed audience. For example, if you were marketing a Jeep when they first came out, you may have assumed that your customer would be an adventurous man. However, unexpectedly, the Jeep proved to be extremely popular with people who live in the city, including teenagers and young mothers. The audience was much larger than initially assumed and led to greater success for jeeps and their 4X4 imitators. This example shows that it's important to listen, observe, and be sensitive to what's happening in the marketplace.

Many companies choose to target audiences in the United States in addition to their local country. For example, a company based in Spain that sells a technology product, would most likely advertise both locally and to the U.S. market. Companies often assume that the U.S. market has the most potential. Some companies have gone against the norm and have benefited greatly, including WhatsApp which got its lift by being widely popular in Brazil, and Viber which is widely used in Russia.

This type of Go to Market (GTM) strategy, while based on assumptions, inevitably establishes the presumed audience. Some companies are so focused on who they believe to be their audience that they fail to find one at all—a common mistake. This insistence may lead to those companies struggling to get their first users. Ultimately, if this approach continues, they will either be recognized only when their audience learns about them organically, or they will fail.

Don't get me wrong, many companies conduct extensive research to determine the presumed audience, but there are additional factors that even the best researchers miss. When assessing audiences, try not to think of specific locations or languages. Instead, think of who your service or product can benefit. Contemplate what other uses your product may have, who can afford it, and who might want it even if they cannot afford the price. Frequently, people with less disposable income get the most expensive gadgets. It depends on the customer's culture and needs.

This brings me to my next point; it's essential to understand which cultures your product might be a good fit for.

Many large industry leaders in one country have failed in others for this exact reason. Take Dunkin Donuts, for example. Americans love donuts, and it is part of their culture to have them with their coffee for breakfast or during breaks. Donuts even come with a stereotype relating to cops. But take it to a country like Israel where it's not part of the culture, and it can easily fail. Dunkin Donuts opened their first location in Tel Aviv in 1996. It was a huge hit at first but quickly withered as the buzz died out and closed in 2001.

Keeping the culture in mind for your target audience is important. They may benefit from or even enjoy using your product, but if it is not culturally feasible, then it might not truly take off for that audience, regardless of how much they may fit your target audience profile in other ways.

Naturally, finding your audiences is easier said than done, and you might have to start off targeting your assumed and presumed audiences. The main point is to keep discovering and listening to your customers and to understand why they buy your products and how they are used.

Additional factors to keep in mind:

- Return on Investment (ROI): You might have the perfect target audience in mind, but reaching it might be too costly and not worth the financial effort. For example, your product might be great for CEOs, but targeting CEOs for the product might end up costing you $200 a sale. If the profit from each unit is under $200, you might sell at a loss. Make sure the return is worth the investment. If you're faced with such a dilemma, look for ways to either cheapen the cost of reaching that audience or find a way to get more for your money such as leveraging the CEOs.

- Timing: Your audience will change with the evolution of your product. What doesn't work for them today, might work tomorrow. So while it makes sense to lower or even stop spending on audiences that don't convert, don't write them off completely.

- Buying Cycle: Are you approaching your audience at the right phase of their buying cycle and with the correct approach? The timing might be right, but the approach may be off. Try and figure out how to segment your messaging to deliver the right information.

- Messaging: Test your messaging and branding constantly, don't give up on an audience until you feel confidant you have tested enough messaging variations.

- Authorship: Has your brand built enough of a reputation that your audience can trust you? Think of your business as you would a dental office. Even if you need a dentist and you are actively looking for one, chances are you won't use the yellow pages. You will look for reviews or ask your friends for recommendations.

- Trends: Is your audience prone to trends? Will they leave as soon as the next big thing comes out? Is your product part of a current or emerging trend? While it makes sense to ride the wave, this is also when your branding will have the most effect on future sales and when you can influence customers in a way that will keep them loyal after the trend passes.

To recap: Reaching a target audience has many phases and requires constant, in-depth analysis. If you are failing to get through to your audience, don't give up on them. Instead, try to assess what is missing.

What factors might you be overlooking? Perhaps the audience simply doesn't fit the current stage that your company or products are in, but that doesn't mean you can't target them later. Perhaps you are reaching out with the wrong messaging. You may want to test multiple messages on various platforms and see if you can make that connection in a different way.

If your issue is authorship, try reaching out to your audience with something of value. Get your audience to investigate your company, stimulate their interest, and reach out to them on social networks before you come to them with your marketing pitch.

Additionally, one of the most important factors is to understand that when you are reaching out to your audience for the first time, you need to do so as if it were a first date or interview. If your audience doesn't get the right picture the first-time round, you may never regain the opportunity for them to form the right impression needed to get them on board.

Regardless of who your audience is, treat them like you would when meeting someone new. Start the conversation by introducing the company. Tell them about the product, the company's background, and your core values. Make a connection. Who knows? You might even end up with a loyal customer.

Since there are so many options when it comes to reaching out to your audience, I find going over some of the fundamentals before I get started is extremely helpful. It minimizes mistakes and prevents me from being led astray by shiny new tools and methods—after all, even marketers get marketed to.

Targeting Methods

Each advertising platform offers its own targeting methods, which enable advertisers to selectively reach their audiences. Targeting methods are not only valuable for the advertiser but are also a primary focus for the advertising platforms success as marketers actively look for new methods. Having new targeting methods come out often shows ingenuity and keeps marketers interested.

To offer targeting methods, advertising platform companies need first to obtain that target audience and be able to categorize it. This is why a company such as Google provides many services for free. For example, Gmail is a free service which is widely used and provides Google with a full array of information about each user. Once you have a Gmail account and you use other Google products, a sort of profile is built for you which places you in various lists for advertising purposes. This and other methods such as partnerships with other companies who hold lists of users with other traceable information allow Google to provide its advertisers with precision targeting.

Additionally, as many use its services, Google can easily provide targeting methods for its own services, such as the search network, the display network, and YouTube.

The search networks enable advertisers to target people searching on Google Search. The display network enables advertisers to reach their target audiences on websites, blogs, forums, and other online properties and place video ads on YouTube.

The main targeting methods are:

- Keyword based, available on search, display, and YouTube

- Placement based, display, and YouTube (includes apps)

- Age and gender on all platforms

- Geo by, country, city, and even zip code radius

- Interest and affinity and in-market audiences

- Retargeting by pages visited

- Similar audiences, a way to reach people with similar characteristics as people who took action on your site (on Facebook known as lookalikes)

- Behavioral such as people with similar purchase history or believed to be early adopters for your targeting

- Household income, which can be useful when targeting products with certain price points, but not necessarily accurate, it really depends on the culture and product. Naturally, if you were selling Ferraris, it would make sense to target people with very high incomes.

There are many other methods as well as combinations, and these keep growing with new and more sophisticated ways to reach users. Some methods of targeting that are not yet available, but I believe will hit the market in the upcoming years are:

- Wearable targeting, for example, people with smart watches, there are some options available, but it's still very limited.

- VR and AR ads will lead to targeting options for people using those technologies, there are companies already offering services, and it will likely grow with the popularity and adaptation of these technologies.

- The weather has yet to be accounted for but plays a role in people's buying habits and is sure to arrive at some point. For example, targeting people with hot soup ads on an abnormally cold day or an add on Waze to buy an umbrella on your route when it suddenly starts raining.

- Mood ads, with more tech available such as Apple Watch which can sense your heart rate and map your health you could start getting ads based on that sort of data.

Targeting: Broad vs. Narrow

There are many factors to consider when approaching an online strategy. A highly targeted campaign might have a high conversion rate, but due to the CPC, be expensive. In comparison, a less targeted campaign might have a poorer conversion rate, yet end up costing the same or less than the highly targeted campaign.

As an example, let's say the product offered is a new health tech one, which can take your blood pressure with one press of a button. Your target audience, in this case, might naturally be people suffering from high blood pressure. You would then create campaigns targeting people searching for related terms, or meds for high blood pressure. You may even use some display placements on relevant sites. This would be the targeted approach, which will generally work well. However, as you are being highly targeted, you are also competing with others trying to reach that same audience, so your CPCs might be high. For this example, let's set the average CPC at $2. After running your campaigns for a few weeks, you realize that on average it takes twenty clicks to get a sale, so for every $40 you spend you make one sale.

A less targeted approach might be to focus on people only by age. For example, after some research, you discover that people over the age of 50 are prone to high blood pressure. You run a campaign targeting only by age. This time your target audience is much bigger and as far as you know, has no interest in finding a product like yours. It now takes 100 clicks to get a single sale. However, as you are not competing for a highly targeted audience, your click now only costs you $0.40. Both campaigns have a similar ROI, but one is highly targeted, and one is less targeted. As with any campaign, you have to try various approaches while keeping an open mind and focusing on ROI. A less targeted campaign might have a less direct effect but could end up getting you cost effective sales and allow you to influence a broader audience.

However, it is important to note, there is a negative aspect to broader targeting. This approach results in bringing a less targeted audience to your site, which also adds them to your remarketing list. The remarketing list is then probably of less quality than if you had only run highly targeted campaigns. However, you can minimize the adverse effect of this with your remarketing settings.

We Are All Early Adopters

Chances are, even if you are new to marketing or sales, you have heard the term "early adopters." What are early adopters? To better understand buyer behavior, potential buyers are segmented into types based on how likely they are to take action. The theory is that as there are a variety of people with different personalities, some are more adventurous when it comes to trying new products, and want to be the first to do so.

Other consumers will only try a product once it becomes a trend, and their friends are using it. Then we have people who will only try it once it becomes part of the culture, and the majority of people are using it. Finally, there are those who will hold out, and sometimes it may be years before they come around, if ever.

An example would be the personal computer, which was introduced in 1977. While some people purchased it because they saw the potential, or simply wanted it right away, it wouldn't become a household item until the mid-1980s. Even throughout the 1990s, there were still individuals using typewriters. Some even prefer that method today, though now it's more of a novelty item than a working piece of equipment. Today, most people can't imagine going a day without their smartphone, tablet, or laptop, which are all variations of the original idea of a personal computer. While some products will never reach this type of mass usage, the possibility of growing into the culture for long-term success is still achievable.

This is the main idea behind Roger's Diffusion of Innovation Bell -- that every product must go through at least three main phases of user types until it can be widely accepted. Early adopters, early majority, and late majority. In other words, the majority of people are not early adopters, but investing in them can lead to the product being further expanded to the early majority, and to the ultimate success, "the late majority", by which time the product is widely accepted.

In today's market, publishers try to measure potential buyers based on this metric, and it enables advertisers to choose early adopters as targeting metrics. Facebook does this by understanding which of their users are most interested in new technologies based on what they like, and what they purchase online. A person who likes the TED page and CNET and also purchases through Facebook ads on a monthly basis may find themselves on an early-adopters list.

What is important to keep in mind is that while people have general traits and behaviors that you might be able to segment them by, each individual also has interests and needs that might make them an early adopter for one product, and a late adopter for others. Essentially we are all both, early adopter and late adopters. Therefore, I find the key is not to search for the mythical early adopter for your product, but rather to find where you are most relevant to your audience. Those who are impressed, in awe, or excited about what you are doing will become your early adopters.

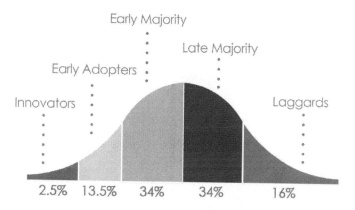

Rogers Diffusion Of Innovation Bell

PhotoBizCoach.com
BeateChelette.com

PART 4:
MESSAGING AND MARKETING MATERIALS

Overview

One of the biggest dilemmas marketers face, and a time consuming one at that, is the creation of marketing materials. These materials can range from a simple text or banner to full-scale websites and landing pages. Once the objective is defined, platforms and target audiences chosen, there are several ways to approach this task. You can create multiple materials and A/B test, you can create them based on your research and sales history, or you can simply go with a hunch.

No matter which way you go, these are fundamentals to keep in mind, or what I like to call the **3 Es**:

- **Educate**: Whether you are targeting people who are not familiar with your brand or long-time customers, you should always try and educate your customers. This can be through basic info about your product or service or with information vital to pique their interest. If you educate, it will resonate! Your audience should be learning something new about your product or service with every communication.

  Educating your audience will not only increase the chance of them taking action, but it will also build trust, move them quickly through the buying cycle and reduce the possibility of them looking up competitors' products. If they do look at competitors' products, but you managed to communicate your product in a better way, you may win the sale even if the competitor has a similar or even better product.

- **Enrich**: Don't only promote your product, add value, show benefits, and provide information which would make your prospects think about your products well after they viewed your promotion. Your content isn't just a bunch of words, images, or videos put together, each image, video, word, and sentence should have a purpose and leave its mark.

- **Enlist**: Get your customers working for you, and turn them into brand ambassadors. Not only will they be great customers, but they will also bring you new customers. When your content is great, people will not only appreciate it; they will share it. Get your customers excited about what you are doing and give them some insight into your company. The more they feel like a part of what you're doing, the more they will want to be a part of it. People like to know that there are real people, history, causes, and culture behind the product.

To achieve all of this with your content, keep it personal. And by personal, I don't mean addressing an email to a person by name; I mean personal to their needs, interests, or passions.

Keep your messaging simple and to the point. You may want your brand to be perceived as sophisticated, but it doesn't mean your messaging can't do that and still be clear and comprehensible to all. Keep your content fresh and captivating. Make sure it's relevant and pulls people in. The point of having marketing materials is not to check a box; it's to dazzle, persuade, influence, and sell.

How to Get People to Feel Your Product

"People will forget what you said, people will forget what you did, but people will never forget how you made them feel."
– Maya Angelo

It is no secret that emotions and primal instinct often fuel the actions people take. We have five main senses: hearing, sight, smell, touch, and taste. For marketing purposes, I will add the sensation of temperature.

Each sense provides us with a piece of information about our surroundings and the combination of these pieces of information form our perceptions. Our perception and emotional state are vital aspects of decision-making. When we see an ad online, we are using our sense of vision. When we see a video or television ad, we use our vision and hearing; this is one reason why many believe video is a stronger means of conveying a message. Simply put, a video engages the viewer with multiple senses and therefore makes a greater emotional impact.

The senses you don't see in online ads are touch, smell, and taste. It can be difficult to truly engage these senses, but if you are able to do so, then your impact will increase. With physical marketing, some fragrance companies overcome this by placing physical scents in their magazine ads, allowing readers to actually smell the fragrance, thereby providing a more significant impact on their potential customer.

I have yet to see an online ad you can taste. However, certain research suggests a person who watches someone run or envisions themselves doing an activity, can actually burn more calories while envisioning it. Our bodies can be tricked into believing false information based on what data our senses provide. Have you ever watched a movie and been frightened when the character was holding onto a ledge for dear life? Even though it was just a film and not happening to you, those heartbeats are completely real.

Do you ever get hungry when you see an ad for pizza on television, even though it's not physically in the room? For some, it's enough to see someone else get injured and they will feel the pain. Senses are the gateway to our emotions. They can evoke happiness, sadness, fear, joy, and stress.

When it comes to marketing, understanding the part played by our senses and emotions is key. The more senses you incorporate it in your brand messaging (and how you do so) will impact the emotional result and deepen the impact it has on your customers either positively or negatively.

Color not only helps us distinguish between objects, but it also plays a significant role in emotional perceptions. Colors are perceived differently by different cultures, which is very important to take into account when targeting globally. For general purposes, however, blue is known to represent trust, red is passion, yellow is a happy color, and black is associated as classic and expensive, and of course let's not forget about green, yes, that's money or success.

Where and how you use these colors can change the audience's perceptions, but one thing is certain colors matter. Some companies have taken this as far as adding elements to their logos. Take Amazon as a perfect example. The yellow arrow knows as a "happy" color, points from A to Z to emphasize the volume of products they offer, and it's shaped like a smile, which is meant to evoke an even stronger positive emotion. Last I checked it seems to be working for them.

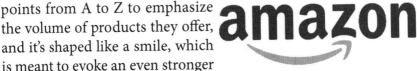

Logo courtesy of Amazon.com

Photograph courtesy of GoDaddy.com

Sex sells—we all know it. But why does it sell? We know we're not getting the model in the ad but are stuck instead with the product. Some may say it has to do with wanting to be like the model, but there's more to it. The model's sex appeal stirs our senses, and the emotion of arousal is what eventually leads us to buy. Yes, we are that primitive!

Subliminal messaging is the practice of inserting a hidden message, which can affect the psyche of its audience. With sensory marketing, the aim is to use senses and emotions to provide the audience with a strong perception of the product. In this way, the audience can not only see the product but also have an associated feeling for it. If done well, the ad will cease to be just a piece of marketing and will become a part of their reality.

Take for example the famous "Got Milk" commercial, showing various people with a milk mustache. This may not be the most appealing picture to look at, but what they did was to take a product in a container and make it real. You could almost taste the milk—just by looking at those ads.

How about this one from Nespresso: Are they selling coffee or sweets? Perhaps they are selling the overwhelming emotion of joy, which comes from looking at all the steamy goodness coming

Photograph by Christopher Badzioch/Getty.

out of the coffee to convey a sense of heat. You can't help but feel the sweetness; even the foam looks more like whipped cream than foam. Throw in some chocolate and red berries for passion, and you have a cup full of emotions ready to be served.

When it comes to temperature, a simple run of water on the bottle is more than enough to convey that the bottle is cold and refreshing. Advertising publishers are yet to add temperature as a geo targeting method, but it is sure to come.

Photograph courtesy of Nespresso

While having an ad that stands out is important, with today's overwhelming number of ads fostering Tunnel Vision Marketing, it is more important than ever to not only tell your story but also to have your audience feel it.

Image courtesy of Coca Cola

Don't get me wrong: I am not saying you need to hit all senses with every ad. Your ads should still make sense and be mindful of branding, but spicing them up with a bit of emotion can go a long way. Whenever you see an ad and the elements don't make sense to you, look closer, not at what you see but at what you feel. You just might understand what they were aiming to achieve if you examine it from an emotional aspect.

Why People Buy Products and Services

Whether you see yourself as more of penny pincher or a shopaholic, we are all consumers. Our consumption falls into a few categories such as necessities, entertainment, work related purchases, and then there is the biggest category for most, which is simply things we want or think we need. Regardless of the category, as emotional buyers, we buy things that are either familiar to us where we know what the outcome will be and how it may make us feel or we buy something we have never owned with an expectation of how it will make us feel.

Understanding what state an individual may be when approaching them is key to nailing the right messaging. If you can place yourself in the buyer's shoes and understand what they would be looking to get from the buyer experience you can tailor your messaging to fit their primal, instinctive triggers.

Here's an example:

John is looking to buy a new car and is searching for an SUV. We could assume he either likes SUVs and this is not his first SUV or that he is expecting a new family and is switching to an SUV from a smaller vehicle. It would be a mistake, however, to build the messaging based on one of these assumptions unless we have a way to know which scenario is taking place. But what we can assume is that buying a new car is an experience. The experience is that you are either buying your first car or moving from something older to something new.

There are no doubt technical aspects that are important when buying a car. For example, safety is very important for those buying an SUV for family purposes. Your selling point should be about how this new SUV will improve the buyer's life, not a list of features. Instead of a sentence such as: "Enhanced safety features," you could use something along the lines of, "Get your hands on the most advanced safety features to hit the market this year." While both may sound similar the first tells you that the car has safety features, the second tells you that you will be moving from what you have now, which is not advanced, to the most advanced safety features on the market.

By showing the potential buyer, not only what they will get but also how it will change their life, you enter a deeper consciousness of the internal buyer's instincts. The SUV itself is a product of understanding where a customer is, what he needs, and how to give him that without the prospect of losing out on what he already has. In the case of the SUV, a common use case is a father who has his pickup truck and now needs to change vehicles to support his growing family needs. Naturally, that is only one audience; it can just as easily be a mother or anyone who simply likes SUVs. The targeting will take the customer type into account, and the messaging will cater to their desires and needs.

Make It Personal, Don't 'Make It Personal'

It is no secret that people like attention. We like it when others know our name or have some personal information about us. This is one of the reasons why so many emails these days have your name in the subject line; it helps improve open rates and makes the email feel personal. Coca Cola even created a series of cans and bottles with widely used names which worked wonders from a sales perspective.

People bought their name, a loved one's name, or a friend's name; but more than that, it also became a social phenomenon, as people took pictures with their coke bottles and posted them to social media. It doesn't matter that there are probably over a million "Daniel's" in

Image courtesy of Coca Cola

the world. When I saw my name on a bottle, it was speaking to me personally; that can of coke literally had my name on it.

While it is challenging to create ads with people's name on them, the next best thing is adding a personal or professional title. For example, if you were targeting doctors with a new innovative tool, your ad could read, "A revolution in medical diagnostics" and it may just get some doctors attention. However, you could revise the ad to read "Doctor, this diagnostics tool is the revolution you've been waiting for!" This revised ad may work better as now you are addressing them on a personal level. I once saw an ad that read "Are you a digital marketer? We have a tool just for you!" I can still recall my first reaction to the ad, which was, " Why yes, I am a digital marketer." I may not have needed their service, but they sure did get my attention.

Another factor to consider when you are trying to connect with potential customers on a personal level is their ego. We all have one, even though some of us may like to think we don't. All it takes is one patronizing ad to realize our egos are in place. For example, our egos may react strongly to an ad that reads, "Digital marketer, lets us teach you how to get it right the first time." That is an ad I have actually seen, and guess what, they did not get the chance to show me how to anything! As soon as I saw that ad, my defenses went up. My inner voice said, "You won't teach me, I'll teach you!" Had the ad read, "Expand your knowledge," I may have looked into it.

Rephrasing the ad and acknowledging that I have skills stirs up my curiosity, whereas dismissing my knowledge and experience simply creates antagonism. It's important to show value to your potential customers, but always respect them and put yourself in their shoes to see how would you react to your own ad.

CTAs And Psychological Triggers

A call to action (CTA) is a text or button placed to get a viewer to take action. It can be anything from a "Buy Now," "Purchase," or "Act Now" for a product, to "Send" for a form, "Sign Up" for a newsletter, and "Read More" for an article. While the CTA is referred to as the main action taken, there are many smaller CTAs placed in the text to help move the viewer in the right direction, and can also be found in product videos.

Many variations come with a CTA: use of color, fonts, and the shape of a button play a role in its click through rate. As previously noted, colors can invoke an emotional trigger making the CTA more appealing to click on. Additionally, the right triggers can help move the entire sale along, meaning there is more than one CTA in a sales funnel. The last trigger is just as important as the first.

In addition to CTAs, there are also various types of psychological triggers. For example, text such as "limited quantity available" which looks to invoke our fear of loss. Many studies have shown that the fear of losing something is a stronger trigger than the will to gain something which is not already yours. Placing a time limit on an item can further increase the urgency. For example, "Limited quantity, sale ends in 3 days." For this to be effective, it should come after the messaging and branding to get the viewer excited about the product.

Another such trigger is "Sold Out." This is used by real estate agents when displaying their other available properties. They leave the sold properties on the board rather than removing them. By adding a "Sold Out" label to them, they take advantage of every possible trigger. What the realtor is doing is conveying to buyers that properties are going fast and they should act now not to lose out. To sellers, this sign says that this realtor can sell. This same tactic is used online, by showing some products as "On Sale," and others as "Sold Out." The message to viewers is to act quickly before these "On Sale" units sell out too.

Free or fast shipping—you see it everywhere these days. Why? Most people don't want to pay extra for something online if they feel they could get it in a store without waiting. So adding the shipping to the cost and giving "Free Shipping" is almost a no brainer.

Some people shop online from necessity and some out of boredom, but one thing most people have in common is that they want to get what they pay for as soon as possible. Fast shipping taps into those needs, and it also helps during holidays or when people are buying a gift and want to be sure it will arrive on time.

We all know that generally, giving makes the giver feel good. Don't get me wrong, I'm all for helping those in need, but the truth is that most people help others because it makes them feel better about their own lives. Without getting too philosophical, I'll jump to the point that having a cause is another great sales trigger. Companies like TOMS, for example, promise that for every pair of shoes you buy, they will donate another pair to a person in need. Let's face it, even with the buy one give one, they are still hugely profitable. They managed to infiltrate one of the most competitive markets in the world by leveraging people's will to give.

With this method, it's not all about the customers; it's also a big PR boost. This doesn't mean that any company who claims to be charitable will succeed. But in a saturated market, giving people a reason to buy from you vs. a competitor can go a long way. And opening your wallet for a pair of shoes you may or may not currently need, becomes easier when attached to the feeling of helping another.

While some may view the main website CTA as the first in the buying cycle, and ads as simply a way to get people to click and visit a site, they are actually much more. They provide the viewer not only with a first impression but also with the first actual CTA. The CTA you choose for your ads has a bigger impact than click through. It sets up the mindset of the visitor. For example, a "Learn More" CTA tells the viewer that there is information about the product or service that they still need to gather before making a decision, priming them to explore your website. Whereas a "Buy Now" CTA tells the viewer, if you like what you see, just go ahead and buy it, or primes them for a possibility of making a purchase.

This does not mean that using "Learn More" can't lead to a sale, or that a "Buy Now" approach will mean more sales. It means you need to evaluate your product and find the best CTA for your product or service. If your product requires a more in-depth review before people purchase, using "Learn More" may help prime visitors to do so. If your product is known, and all the viewer needs to do is choose and buy, then "Buy Now" may work better.

Naturally, there are many other CTAs you can use, including: "Discover," "Pre-Order," "Get," and "Donate," etc. The idea is to experiment and find the one that works best for your product or service. Understanding that your ads are more than just ads, but actually fuel the action taken on your site, can go a long way to perfecting your messaging.

Find Your WOW Factor

The term "wow moment," reflects a time of an epiphany, or when you are suddenly overtaken with excitement. When you manage to deliver your viewers a wow moment, your conversion rate will rise, and your buying cycle can be dramatically shortened. With attention spans being incredibly short these days and visitors to your site deciding to stay on your site in seconds, the sooner you manage to deliver this to your audience the better.

You can try to do this in your ads, or on your landing page, preferably above the fold. I know you are probably wondering how do you find your wow factor, and how do you deliver it. Well, it depends on your product. Generally speaking, you need to ask yourself what is your unique value proposition (UVP), and what about it is special enough to make it enticing?

A few years ago, when SimilarWeb, the BI tools, was new to the market, a sales rep came to visit my boss and me to offer us this great new analytics tool. He spent an hour showing us information about our own website, jumping from one data point to the other. We were highly unimpressed and finally stopped his pitch and told him that we already use Google analytics and we didn't see the value or additional benefit that this tool presents. At that point he laughed and said, "Sure you know all these stats about your website, but I can show you the same stats about your competitors' websites, how much traffic they get, where the traffic comes from".

That was our wow moment. We jokingly yelled at him. By showing us our own site for an hour, instead of showing us data about our competitors, he had wasted time in explaining the wow factor of the tool. If the same pitch had been on a website, no doubt we would have left after 30 seconds.

Once we understood what we were seeing and were dazzled by it, we signed on for a trial period on the spot. Your product's information and benefits are all important, but finding your wow factor and highlighting it can seal the deal in moments.

PART 5:

HOW TO STICK THE LANDING

Overview

When you run digital campaigns, the landing page (LP) is any destination you choose to send your audience to once they click on your ads. It can be as simple as your website, a custom page, or even your app store page. Depending on what you offer and how many products you have, you may have only a site or multiple landing pages setups for each product to give your audience a better experience by showing them content related directly to your ad.

Your landing pages are your most important assets and usually are the best-maintained pages in terms of information, links, and calls to action. It doesn't matter how well your ads perform if your landing page has issues. It's just like a real store—you can hand out thousands of flyers, and get hundreds of customers to walk through your door. But if they enter and are disappointed or feel misled, they simply won't buy. This is a first impression that also cannot easily be changed once your target audience members have been turned off.

Sending customers to a bad landing page is a waste of your efforts and money. Just as a good experience leaves a good impression and positive feedback, a bad one may cost you not only the money you invested in the campaign but in the long run, will cost you bad online reviews and bad impressions that linger in your target audience. The days when a bad review in the newspaper would disappear and people would forget are long gone. Online reviews can last forever, and the bad ones will pop up again and again. Your landing page needs to be spot on to give the best first impression possible every time it's clicked on.

How do you know your LP will perform well? The only real way to know is to test it, but if you follow these best practices you will undoubtedly improve your chances of building a great landing page (LP):

- Make sure your LP is related to the ads. People clicking on an ad should get to a page with the same vibe, messaging, and branding. This is not only important for the user experience but will also improve your quality score on platforms such as AdWords.

- Page speed is one of the most important factors. No one wants to wait for your page to load. Seconds matter here, even a four-second delay could cost you a large chunk of visitors abandoning your site.

- Be very clear with your messaging. Don't use phrases that sound cool but mean nothing such as, "Unique Solutions for Everyone." People should know what you offer straight away. If you can't understand what you are selling or offering from that sentence, don't expect others to understand.

- Have a clear call to action (CTA). Most people won't do an action unless they are guided to do so.

- Position elements wisely. There are a few methods such as the "Z" method, which takes into account how we naturally read a page. Place some thought into what viewers should see first and where to place your CTAs.

- Choose colors wisely. The colors can have a direct impact on users' emotions. Set the right mood for your customers. Even the colors in the background images you choose can affect the mood.

- Keep the most critical information and offer above the fold (the visible part of the site without scrolling as soon as a user enters).

- Provide information but limit the user's need to click multiple times to get to more info. If the information is in another tab or page, you must assume it will not be viewed. Your main page info, therefore, must contain the relevant info and pitch, as well as your call to action.

- Provide benefits of using your product or service, not just a sales pitch. Educate your customers about your product or service.

- When possible, make sure you use trust-building elements such as testimonials from some of your clientele and press mentions.

- Have an offer, don't just build awareness. They are already on your LP, now make them an offer they can't refuse. Adding limits on your offer can help, such as "First 50 buyers" or "Limited to..." Make sure all your LPs have conversion tracking pixels and remarketing pixels set up.

- Test each element and make sure it performs as needed. Even the best LP won't help you if filling out a form doesn't work.

- Keep it lean. Your landing page should only contain information that is focused and helps the viewer reach the desired action. It should not be cluttered with anything that does not support the goal. Especially harmful are unnecessary links or tabs shifting focus away from the conversion funnel.

A/B Testing Your Landing Pages

"If you do what you've always done, you'll get what you've always gotten."
– Tony Robbins

A/B testing is used by marketers to test individual elements against others. The testing can be used for a small change such as the color of a button, to larger items such as whole landing pages. The idea is to create at least two landing pages and send an equal amount of traffic to both pages; you then track the traffic and see which page performs best.

For A/B testing to be accurate, it is important to make one change at a time so you can understand what worked and to make sure you send similar traffic and not two different types of targeting. A/B testing is a big part of a landing page's success. Many companies invest heavily in testing various elements on their LPs. They will make small changes, like changing the color of a CTA button, or moving elements around to see the effect. One common mistake is continuing to A/B test an LP that is not converting well, without considering the elements might not be the issue. The issue could be the template design, the load time, or any of the above-mentioned points.

If your LP has a very low conversion, any change you make to a single button will only take you so far. Understanding the key issue is critical to improving performance. Test the full funnel. Mark optional issues for testing, hold a test group or any other method as needed. If all else fails, don't be stubborn. Accept that the page has failed and start from scratch. Remain flexible and test new ideas and new formats. Keep in mind that what you think will work won't always be the case. Get as many eyes on your LP and opinions as possible and get to the heart of what is and isn't working. After all, this is one of your main links to move your potential client or buyer to the next level of the buying cycle, moving them forward to hopefully become a return client.

A poor converting landing page can be an issue of messaging, perception, or disappointment. Imagine you see a great looking advert for an advanced drone, with the text "Take your flying to the next level." Excited by what you read on the ad, you click through to the website only to find a page that looks nothing like the ad. Instead of giving you more information on how you can take your flying to the next level, you are greeted by some basic tech specs and a "buy now" button. Your experience went from excitement and a thirst for more information to complete disappointment. Now imagine that same situation but this time the "buy now" button is green rather than red, would that really make a difference? Perhaps it would. However, I would argue that there are more significant changes needed to this landing page.

Checkout Pages and Cart Abandonment

There are many reasons someone would reach a checkout page, aside from the obvious, which would be to make a purchase. Some do so out of curiosity, others window shop (it's online, so it's more like webshop). Many people add things to the cart to later evaluate if they really want them, and some even get there by mistake, clicking the checkout link.

How people get to the checkout page differs by site and can also change the intent of the viewer. However, one thing is sure; cart abandonment is a huge factor for all e-commerce businesses. While in some cases it can't be helped, there are elements you can work on to reduce the abandonment percentage of your cart. Just like a landing page, a cart needs to be very focused. The customer has already chosen the item(s) they want, so the checkout process should be simple and quick to complete. Any obstacle in the way of the purchaser, and every second they spend before clicking "complete order" is one in which they may change their mind or get distracted.

The elements your cart should have are ones that give the buyer trust and confidence, such as site security badges and secure payment methods. If you have upsell options that can either work in your favor or against you, meaning you may gain in upsold product but lose other sales, this can be A/B tested. Additionally, there are products on the market, for example, AbandonAid and HotJar, which provide advertisers with tools to understand where the drop off is and re-engage the lost users via email, or with your remarketing ads. Naturally, knowing what causes your audience to fall off in the first place is the best way to optimize your sales funnel. Many marketers look at the checkout as a set function or one with little leg room for improvement, but small elements can go a long way.

For example, if you have an offer on your homepage, reinforce it in your cart. If your website has a distinct look and feel, it should be carried through to the cart. Just because it's a cart page does not mean your customers should be yanked out of your website and placed on a stale page.

Imagine if you were shopping at a physical store with some light music in the background, marble floors, perfect lighting and a warm, inviting feeling, and then when you wanted to pay for the things you chose in that setting, you were sent to the cold dark basement. How many people would even reach the basement floor?

Keep Your Customers Delighted

We all experience certain pain points in our daily lives, from videos which take what feels like forever to load, to unnecessary traffic jams, lines at restaurants, and the list goes on. As a proud Xbox owner, I can attest that while I enjoy my playtime, waiting for a new game to load, or even waiting between scenes during a game is nothing less than painful. Many websites have these pain points too. While in some cases there is not much from a technical point that can be done, you can still use that pain point to your advantage by turning it into a delight.

Imagine you just chose a new pair of sneakers off a fashion website. You click to go to the cart, and suddenly you get that awful thinking wheel; it may be a short delay, but it puts you straight into a state of anxiety. What if, instead, while the page was loading, the shoes you chose came alive and started running around the screen? Wouldn't this make the delay a little less irritating, and stop you from questioning your purchase?

The point is, if you can identify these moments in your product, which may be "painful" to viewers, you can work with your development, and product teams to turn these moments into positive ones, enhancing the shopping experience, and making it a delight for your customers.

PART 6:
KEEPING YOUR EYE ON THE PRIZE

Overview

When it comes to business and marketing, there are probably more hype words, KPIs, acronyms, and strategies than there are stars. There are more than enough to make anyone confused, and a confused marketer is one who finds themselves constantly doubting and changing direction. This can only lead you down a path of mayhem, wasting valuable time and resources trying to figure things out.

In the marketing and advertising industry, there are two main terms used to define success, these are, Return on Investment (ROI) and Return on Ad Spend (ROAS). While most people will use these terms interchangeably, we can distinguish between the two. ROI refers to your revenue minus the cost of ad spend, divided by cost. ROAS simply takes your ad spend divided by cost.

Why does it matter? Well, if I was calculating ROAS and my ad spend was $100, and my

revenue was $1,000, I would simply divide them, and my ROAS would be $10 or 1,000% return. If I calculated ROI, I would take into account the dollar spent, and my return would be $9 or 900%.

To truly monitor your success in online marketing, I believe that ROI should always be your focal point as ROI is the only metric that paints a real picture to help you aim for a successful and profitable online marketing strategy. It shows you your true return and helps you focus on profitability. There are instances when your objective might be purely branding, in which case financial ROI might not be your focus. In these cases, your branding should be looked at as your ROI. Look for KPIs, which can help you determine what platform performs best for your branding.

While branding may be hard to quantify, a good hint is usually organic traffic surges to your website. A rise in organic traffic may signify that word of mouth has increased around your product and people are taking notice. Fine-tuning your online branding campaigns for audiences who spend more time on your website, and visit multiple pages can help expand the word of mouth effect even further, and can also result in better on-site conversions. In other words, first, figure out what ROI means to you, then put all your effort and thinking towards reaching that ROI goal.

Understanding Tracking to Reach Your Goals

One of the most challenging aspects of success in online marketing is tracking. It sounds simple enough. You need to track which marketing channels are working and delivering your ROI, and which are not. To track your campaigns and get actionable insights, it's critical to understand how tracking actually works. If you don't understand tracking or don't set it up correctly, there can be disastrous consequences.

Conversion tracking is generally code based. You place a code snippet on a "Thankyou" page. Once an individual clicks on your ad and takes an action such as a purchase or filling out a form and then reaches the "Thankyou" page, that code fires and reports back to the platform that a conversion took place.

Depending on the platform, the information you get back may tell you not only that a conversion took place, but also which keyword, ad, ad group, and campaign it came from. This data then helps you to optimize your campaigns by tweaking elements which aren't performing as well, or even removing them and shifting the budget to better performing ads. This is the basis of conversion tracking. But when it comes to tracking, there is much more to it, and a lack of focus or understanding can really impact your campaigns.

Here are some of the important factors that are helpful to keep in mind:

- Tracking is code based and implementing the pixel correctly is crucial. Poorly implemented pixels will give you false information. If this happens, you are then acting off false data and any optimization as a consequence will be more damaging to your campaign. As a result, you may end up pausing well-performing campaigns as you will not know they are performing well or adding more budget to poorly performing campaigns. In most cases this setup can be done by the marketer but help from a developer maybe needed

- While this may seem obvious, before starting your campaigns make sure the pixel was not only set up correctly but on the right pages as well. Because the pixel reports conversions, it should only fire when a person reaches the "Thankyou" page. I have witnessed situations where the code was placed on the home page by mistake, and each time someone visited the home page the pixel would fire and the ad platform would count it as a sale.

  Needless to say, that was not a productive way of optimizing campaigns. In addition to setting up the conversion pixel on your site's "Thankyou" page you must also make sure the conversion settings in the platform of choice are set up correctly.

- Each platform has a tracking window or a segment of time in which the code will attribute a sale. For example, let's say I clicked on the ad yesterday, but only bought the item today. The platform may still attribute that sale as coming from the ad. Some track 7 days, 14 days, 30 days, or more.

  Some platforms enable you to choose the time frame of the window. Knowing what that window is will help you in comparing performance to other platforms, as different platforms have a default setting of a certain number of days. To avoid having gaps between the data in the different platforms, e.g., AdWords presents a seven-day data, and Google Analytics a twenty day one, it is important to be aware of the setting and align the time frame on each platform.

- When setting up your account on different platforms, it is important to be aware of the time zone you choose. In some platforms, after the initial setup, you can no longer change the setting. This is important, as you do not want to have different accounts in different time zones, as this will skew your information.

- Most purchases of products are not impulsive. The buyer may click on a few ads before the actual purchase takes place. Individuals may not even click the ad, but only see it, and later look for the website directly. On AdWords for instance, a purchase from someone who only saw your ad, but did not click on it, is called a view-through conversion. A person who did click an ad, but then clicked another ad a few days later from a different campaign, would be counted as a conversion on the last clicked campaign, and as an assisted conversion on the first clicked campaign.

- Some campaigns might not bring direct sales; however, they assist in bringing sales to other campaigns. These campaigns can be a vital part of an overall strategy. Keeping your goals simple, focusing on ROI, and understanding how to attribute campaign results to that ROI, are what makes a sustainable online strategy.

Analytics, BI, and Insights: Getting Excited About Data

If you are a marketer or in the field, the term "Data Driven" may have already driven you crazy.

In today's world, where everything you do online is trackable and quantifiable, data is what it's all about. While most marketers believe they are the ones making data driven decisions, while in a sense true, the process itself starts way before the marketer even builds their first campaign.

Almost all platforms these days are programmatic and built around data. For example, if you are running a B2B campaign, you don't choose to advertise on LinkedIn simply because it's a professional network. You use it for the ability to target users by title, profession, seniority, and industry. The marketer's job is not to find these users in a haystack, but rather to choose which platform and which methods to use.

This, however, does not mean that the marketer has no role in improving and finding new ways to target the audience. It simply means they are not starting from scratch. One of the best things about using a platform such as AdWords or Facebook is that with time you can get insights into who your target audience really is, and find information to help you hone in on new potential customers. Google Analytics is one of the most widely used tools for various reasons. The first is, it was one of, if not the first to market. Also, as with many Google tools, it's completely free.

Where your advertising platforms can give you great insights into your purchased user base, analytics can give you additional info into the organic visits, and how people use and interact with your site. SimilarWeb, a paid BI tool, gives marketers the ability to see the same analytics stats they get from their own Analytics account, but for competitor websites (AppAnnie does this for apps). By grouping all of these data points, you can gain valuable insights to improve and expand your marketing efforts.

Let's look at an example of how this can be achieved. Imagine that your company sells car insurance and as such you are in a highly competitive field. First, you create your website with your offer, explaining why your insurance is better than others. Then you start with search campaigns for anyone searching for car insurance related keywords. You may even buy keywords for people looking to buy new cars, as they will no doubt need insurance.

Additionally, you may choose keywords related to accidents, as someone who has been in an accident and is unhappy with their insurance might be primed to move to yours. Next, you start running display ads on various placements related to cars, new cars, and the search targeting. You may even start promoting your new social pages to people who like other insurance pages, or car dealership pages, etc.

Next, you make a list of all your competitors, or at least the local ones, and run them through a BI tool. Getting insights such as traffic they receive, referral traffic, and other goodies. Using the referral traffic insights, you now find a bunch of sites that send traffic to your competitors' sites, keywords that they are buying, and organic keywords used to reach those competitors' sites. You now visit these referral sites and see what options you have to place your ads on those sites. It could be that they have AdSense, Media.com ads, or another option, or they may offer direct media buying options.

You can even put those sites through the BI tools. You now have a network of placements which are all part of your competitors' traffic. You are now buying the same Keywords they are, and others they have yet to find. This puts you directly in action, both competing with your competitors and overtaking them.

Next, you turn to your platform insights and analytics. From the "purchase list" insights you learn that most of the insurance purchasers are age 45 and up and are parents. You also learn they love travel and sales. These insights allow you to further improve both your targeting and offering. Now you move to analytics, where you find that the bounce rate on one of your pages is very high and the conversion rate is low. Another page you are testing has a lower bounce rate and a high conversion rate. You shift your traffic to that page and improve sales by 30 percent.

This was, of course, a made-up scenario, and I must admit, that I have yet to market car insurance. But, hopefully, it gives you a glimpse of what can be achieved with the right set of tools and utilizing data.

The most important takeaway is that marketing today is just as much about tracking as it is about targeting, it's about having quantifiable data and being able to understand the full benefit of your marketing efforts. Some may argue that there is added branding value to online marketing which cannot easily be quantified; however, you can still access your direct impact and make decisions based off that. With the right tools and methods, you can better understand your own data and learn from your industry and competitors to refine and grow your online presence

Metrics: The Key to the Kingdom

When evaluating campaigns or even organic traffic to your site or app, there are hundreds of data points and metrics you can look at to assess performance. Some metrics, however, can provide you with a clearer picture as they hone in on user behavior. One of the most looked at metrics is click through rate (CTR). A CTR is the ratio of people who click on a specific ad to those that viewed it.

CTR can give you an understanding of how interesting or clickable your ads are. However, a click through rate will only tell you if people feel compelled to click an ad, not if they are interested in your actual product. For example, clickbait is a term used for ads and links that compel a person to click on them by means of a misleading text or images. Clickbait ads have the goal of getting as many people as possible to click on them.

For your CTR to really mean something, your ads need to lead to a high conversion rate. Your conversion rate is the percent of people who take action on your site. An ad with a high CTR but a low conversion rate (CVR) could mean one of two things: either the ad has a clickbait element in it or the landing page is not compelling. Your ad could have a clickbait element in it even if that was not your intention. Or perhaps your ad is fine, but the issue is with your landing page. Running multiple ad copies and concepts will help you to understand the issue better. To assess the effectiveness of the various campaign components, you should run a number of ads to the same audience, in the same campaign, which leads to the same landing page (A/B test).

If you see an abnormal discrepancy between different click through rates and conversions for different ads, then a number of things may be going on:

- If the ads have a high CTR but a low conversion rate, then your ads' messaging is likely off.

- If the ads have a low CTR and a high conversion rate, then the targeting is likely off or perhaps the message is not compelling enough.

- Assuming you have a compelling product, but if all ads have low conversion rates, then the landing page or the targeting is most likely at fault

- If you have a high CTR and a high conversion rate, then your ads and landing page are on point.

Many marketers use various landing pages as a way to cater to different audiences, and they can also be used to better understand what works best for your product. A well-balanced and diverse mix of ads and landing pages can help you to understand what works and what doesn't.

There are other metrics, however, which are just as important to look at within a particular ad network, such as reach and frequency.

Frequency is a metric that shows you how many times, on average, single users have seen your ads. A score of below one usually signifies that your ads are doing well and reaching new users as they run. However, once you pass the one point, you are essentially starting to show your ads to the same people over and over again. This can mean a few things: Either your ad has reached all intended users, or you chose a bidding option which limits your reach to only part of your segment. If the latter is true, increasing your bid should help you reach the rest of your audience and lower the frequency.

But why is a higher frequency an issue? First of all, if you bombard users with your ads, they may quickly turn into spam. Users can mark your ads as spam, and if they do, Facebook, for example, will penalize you by charging more for each click/impression. Additionally, if you keep targeting the same audience, those who have already clicked as they were interested in your ad have no reason to do so again. Those who haven't clicked are less likely to do so, resulting in a huge drop in CTR. This will also result in your ads costing more.

Using a large ad platform, such as Facebook, has many perks. However, with so many people on the platform, Facebook needs to allow advertisers to focus on their target audiences. This presents two key issues. First, many companies presume they know who their audiences are but don't always get it completely right at first. Secondly, even if you do know exactly who your audience is, there are endless ways and options for reaching them. For example, you can target by interest, location, title, likes, lookalikes, connections, and more. Add to those elements such as timing and seasonality, and the offer or messaging used, and it's easy to see why marketers get lost on their journey to Facebook success.

With so many variations and variables, no two campaigns will act the same. Even if you run the same exact campaign with the same targeting and ads, the results will differ. Additionally, your ad's performance will change over the duration of its lifetime.

But with so many variables and so much going on, how do you keep your campaigns in check?

Fortunately, there are metrics that allow you to quickly understand a campaign's performance and to take the appropriate actions. Facebook's algorithm works similarly for organic traffic as it does for paid traffic. If your ad's click through rate is low, it means that people are not interested enough in the content. If it's an organic post, it will be limited by Facebook and won't show to all your fans. If it's a paid post, you will receive a low relevance score, which will increase your CPC/Impression costs. So, if you start running a campaign and you see the CTR is poor, you most likely made a mistake either with targeting or the ad itself, and so you need to stop the campaign and reevaluate.

With Facebook, reach is also very important. The more audience you have in your targeting list, the longer it will take to reach a high frequency, assuming your bid is high enough. For most Facebook campaigns, choosing CPM or OCPM will take care of that and tends to perform better than CPC bidding. A well-performing Facebook campaign is one that starts off with a high CTR, remains at a stable frequency throughout its lifetime, and reaches all users evenly. It should be turned off or completed when the frequency starts rising and/or the CTR starts dropping. And of course, here as well, it all comes down to conversion rates and ROI.

For businesses with a recurring user base, such as an app, or a subscription model, it is also important to be aware of the existing client base. Churn is a metric used to quantify the abandonment by clients. Every business experiences churn on some level. With apps, it can be people who uninstall your app or even stop using it. For a company, like eBay, it can be a shopper who stops visiting the site. Churn rate is a percent of this decline. Generally, you will look at churn on a weekly, monthly, and yearly basis. Churn happens most often with newly acquired users/clients but occurs throughout the entire client/user base.

There are many ways to combat churn, from remarketing to keeping your user base engaged and offering incentives to return to your app or store. The most important aspect of churn is understanding that it exists, how it affects your business, and why it's occurring. Armed with that information you can build a retention plan and quantify its success by reducing the churn rate.

Buying Cycles and Seasonality

You can perfect your campaign, set up all of your tracking methods, research your competition, and yet there are still many reasons people will hold off buying a product. Why does this happen? Some of it has to do with natural buying cycles; we all go through a process when purchasing. That process can vary based on factors like whether we have bought this product in the past; is it a necessity, like groceries, or is it something we just desire like a new car or headphones. No matter what it is we buy, first, we think about it, "Do I need it? Should I get this product? How many should I get?"

Additionally, there are external factors including seasonality. Sales go up during Christmas—that's a fact. People buy gifts, look for deals, and fill their house with food and decorations. Most companies will see a rise in sales in December.

But it's not only holidays that mark seasonality. Depending on the product, people may prefer buying something during another specific season. For example, some people prefer buying during known sales dates, such as Memorial Day, Bank Holidays, Black Friday, or Cyber Monday. And of course, there are the yearly seasons, such as camping and cookout equipment in the summer or ski equipment and boots in the winter.

Consequently, when the weather doesn't change when it's supposed to, sales suffer. Some days and hours can see better sales than others for a multitude of reasons. The volume of sales may vary according to when people are at work, and if they have received their pay check yet, or how close they are to the end of the month when the credit card bills start stacking up.

While there are limited things a marketer can do about buying cycles and seasonality, understanding what is affecting your sales can help you plan for it. Improving messaging and offers during those times may also help. This isn't done only online. Take the US restaurant chain, Sizzlers, for example. They offer seniors and students 20 percent off if they come before 6 PM. Sizzlers knows that these demographics probably eat early anyway, and Sizzlers wants to fill up the restaurants during those relatively dead hours. So they offer a deal which makes it appealing for these groups to come in then and charge the full price for families who come in for dinner after 6 PM. The online concept is the same.

For example, if you have days with fewer sales perhaps those are the days you should send your emails out with offers or have a sale on the site that's known to happen only on those days.

Most importantly, knowing what your buyer cycle and seasonality looks like can help you keep calm and not panic when sales suddenly drop. One of the worst things an online marketer can do is to start panicking when sales suddenly dip. If this leads to them changing all their campaigns, bids, and budgets, then this can lead to perfectly well-performing campaigns being disrupted. This will, in turn, make them perform worse once the seasonality changes.

How can you tell if its seasonality or not? It's not always as clear as Christmas, Black Friday, or Cyber Monday. In many cases, if you see a sudden drop in sales and don't have previous year or months data to compare to, you can usually find information online, such as forums where others in your industry are voicing the same concerns or research conducted about that time of year and volume of sales.

Part 7:
From Plan to Execution

Overview

While there are many aspects of digital marketing, one of the most prominent is running online campaigns. Every great battle that was ever won started not with the first soldier to charge, but with the General miles away planning each move. A strong leader understands the strengths of their forces and how to best use them, and knows that each battle-ready element has its purpose, benefits, and limitations, and uses them in harmony at the correct time. The digital marketing strategy does exactly that.

Once you understand who your audience is and what the objectives are, you then need to understand your resources, budgets, and assets required. You'll also need to determine if you have enough time to gather the assets you want. Next, plan your course of attack, platform, messaging, call to action (CTA), length of campaign, and decide if you can test the waters first or go in full force.

The stages are:

- **Research and Planning**: Plan your campaigns based on the budget you have and the outlets available to reach your target audience. Keep in mind that this also means choosing the best bang for your buck. It's not about being on all platforms and showing up everywhere; it's about selecting the platforms that will provide you the best ROI. Sometimes you will have to test various platforms to determine what works. For this reason, your budget should be split up into an ongoing budget and a test budget.

I like to keep a 20 percent ratio of test budget on an ongoing basis so I can keep testing, learning, and scaling. A larger percentage will generally be needed during the first few months. Once you understand who your target audience is and have selected the platforms, the research phase can also include gathering data regarding these outlets, such as pricing, possible reach, and materials needed. Once you understand all of this, you may have to adjust your budget accordingly.

- **Campaign Creation**: While building a great strategy is key to your overall success, creating your campaigns are equally important. They must be built well with great attention to detail and must follow the strategy. It's easy to get led astray during the building phase, so it's important to keep focused and have the main structure blocked out before you start building campaigns.

- **Content Creation:** Your campaigns need to focus on content that will not only get your message out to your target audience but also capture their attention. This phase requires its own planning to make sure your messaging is cohesive and aligned with your campaign goals and target markets. You should do this by working with a content marketer, a copywriter, and a graphic designer when possible.

- **Deployment**: Once your campaigns are ready, deployment is usually as easy as clicking a mouse, but it's also your last chance to review all the settings in the campaign and cross referencing them to your goal. If they all align, great. Click the switch. But you may find some hidden setting or some unnoticed ones, which may have made sense at the time of creation, but no longer do. Whenever you start a new campaign or renew a paused one, you should go over the settings, the ads, the links, and make sure it is all correct and working.

- **Observation**: Deployment is only the beginning of a campaign. The hard work starts once the campaigns are active and you are observing the interactions. Is your target audience engaging with your content? If they are and there is a high CTR, what are the types of responses you are receiving? Are they doing the actions you are after? Are there any areas where you can improve your content based on the feedback received? This is a trick question. You can always improve, and if you think you can't, look again!

- **Optimization**: Ask any marketer, and the word optimization is like reminding them they need to breathe. The constant question on your mind should always be, what else can I try, and how can this be better? Optimization is not so much a single stage, as it is a daily routine.

- **Reporting**: Throughout this process, you will be collecting data based on clicks, content engagement, and the overall responses from your target audience. Depending on what your end goal is, you can determine whether or not your campaign is achieving that goal. The reporting stage holds you accountable because it is a measure of the results of your efforts. If you have done the hard work throughout the other stages, these reports should be a sign of the success of those efforts. While reporting can be a daunting task, it is crucial both for the optimization and achieving true ROI.

When it comes to reporting, however, it is also important to understand what time frame is reasonable for handing in a report. Some managers may want a report daily or weekly, depending on the buying cycle. Platforms using a report like that may give skewed results. For example, if you hand in a daily AdWords report and return to those campaigns a week later, you will sometimes find that additional conversions were added as AdWords was counting conversions up to 30 days. If the buyer cycle is two weeks and you give a daily report or even a weekly report, you will most likely not be able to give sales numbers in that report. This does not mean you should ignore or deny the manager's wishes; however,

I find it critical that all involved understand the limitations and agree on how each data point will be evaluated. In this case, for example, the daily might only be used to monitor impressions, clicks, and CTR, and the monthly would be used for an overall understanding.

When reviewing campaigns, you can't simply look at one factor to make a call. All pieces need to fit together for it to work. By creating reports and looking at all the available metrics, you can achieve the insight needed to make calls that can lead to better optimization.

The Importance of Campaign Settings

When creating campaigns, regardless of the platform, understanding the settings is crucial. I know it sounds obvious, but sometimes the smallest misunderstanding can cost you dearly. For example, when you run an AdWords search campaign targeted at the U.S., you need to go then and select English as your language setting, especially if your keywords are in English. Of course, that makes perfect sense, but AdWords targets language based on the operating system settings. This means that if a person's operating system is in Spanish, they will not see your ads, even if they speak or understands English perfectly. Not only that, but search campaigns are keyword based, so the individual would have to actively search for those words or similar phrases for your ads to show.

Therefore, it shouldn't matter what language their operating system is set to. If they are looking for your keywords, they should be able to find you. The best setting in this case and with any keyword-based search campaign would be to use "all languages" as the language setting choice.

But why is this setting so important? Well, it's not only about losing out on the users searching for your keywords, but also about narrowing down the audience. When using a different OS language, it also ends up costing you more per click since your ads are now more targeted leading to higher competition. Depending on your marketing objectives, it may be more important to gather a broader audience versus narrowing down to a specific language.

Frequency capping is another critical setting. Using this method only in display campaigns, you can limit the number of times a unique user (1 person) can see your ads. Selecting a frequency cap of three per campaign and per day would mean that any person who sees any ad in that campaign could only be exposed to it three times a day. Frequency capping is best used when your target audience is small, and there is a fear of spamming users to the point where they not only ignore your ads, but dislike them, or start considering them abusive and sometimes even reporting them.

The most important place to use frequency capping is with your remarketing campaigns, which are targeting those individuals who previously reached your landing page but did not make an actual purchase. These people are still potential buyers, so every impression needs to leave them with a positive impact.

With display campaigns, you have an option to target by keyword; this is great as it means your ads could show up anywhere on the web where your keyword appears. For example, if you are selling a drone, you could choose the keywords drone, drones, etc., and your drone ad would show up based on those words. However, when creating this type of campaign and adding your keywords, there are two targeting options. You can choose either "Content" or "Audience."

Keyword setting ?   ● **Audience:** Show ads to people likely to be interested in these keywords and also on webpages, apps, and videos related to these keywords (recommended)
○ **Content:** Only show ads on webpages, apps, and videos related to these keywords

The content option means that your ads will only show on sites where the exact words you chose appear in the actual text. The audience option means it will show up on any website based on whether the audience is most probably interested in that keyword, meaning it would be enough that they previously visited a site with that keyword to be on your list, but not necessarily looking at a relevant article or webpage at the moment.

This is a huge difference. The pre-selected option is **audience**, as it gives AdWords the broadest option to advertise, but this doesn't mean the results will be in your favor. Depending on the type of product, you may want to test both options separately, but it's easy to go with the default setting and overlook the one that is probably what you were aiming to achieve.

There are many settings, and they don't always mean, and act the same way on different platforms. While it may be time-consuming to dive deep and learn all of them, it will certainly be worth your while in the long term. Imagine if you ran a campaign for one month, and due to a setting misunderstanding, got 50 sales that month when you might have gotten 70 with the correct setting. If 50 would leave you with a negative ROI, you would simply pause that campaign or optimize it. But if 50 would be an acceptable ROI, you would essentially miss out on 20 extra sales that month. Now imagine if this is a campaign you run for a year.

We are all human, and as such, make mistakes. When a campaign fails to reach your objectives, never assume it's simply a bad campaign. Always double-check the settings, the ads, the target audience and so on before jumping to conclusions. As a consultant, many times I will be asked to review campaigns built by other marketers and, more often than not, the issues I find are not in the build or type of campaigns, but with very simple settings that were misused. A simple click can sometimes make the difference between success and failure.

Budgeting

"A mathematical confirmation of your suspicions"
–A.A Latimer

While it would be amazing to have an endless budget, most companies allocate a specific budget to their online campaigns. When it comes to online marketing, budgeting decisions can be one of the most decisive factors governing your overall outcome. The budget can not only influence your reach and how many campaigns you can build and test, but can also affect the campaigns themselves. For example, if a CPC is around $1.5 and your budget is only $10 a day you could only afford to get six clicks, and you will be limited not only by the actual budget but by the algorithm. The recommended budget is usually around 100 times your bid, in this case, $150.

People tend to look for equal numbers and balance; we prefer to bid in jumps of whole numbers such as $0.50, $1, $1.50 rather than $0.51 or $0.52, etc. The same is true for budgeting; it's easier for us to set a budget of $100 than one of $104. But whole numbers might not always be the optimal way to go. This is especially true with CPC as over time every cent counts. If you can save $0.05 while getting the same results on each keyword and you get a few thousand clicks a day, those sums can be very meaningful.

One of the biggest questions when budgeting is how to spread out your budget. Most companies plan their budgets monthly, quarterly, and yearly and operate under monthly budget restraints. This type of budgeting seeps into the marketing departments as well. While it is understandable to have an overall monthly budget for Marketing, spreading that budget evenly over the whole month (daily) is not always the best course to take.

Let's say your monthly budget for June was $5,000, if you were to divide it daily, you would have $166 per day for all your campaigns, this could be very limiting if you have many campaigns to test. One approach would be to start the month out with a higher portion of the budget and then lower it based on results. Additionally, you could choose to spend your whole budget in the first week and not over the full month, giving you a higher daily budget needed to test your campaigns well.

Naturally, this is not recommended for all cases. For instance, if your business is a physical one and you are sending traffic to the location, you may want to keep it spread out over the month, or on slow days, if your campaigns perform better on certain days, you may want to use your budget mainly on those days.

There are many points to take into account when budgeting. What I find most important is to look at your overall goals and the type of business, and then create a budgeting plan which takes those and the platforms used into account, rather than conforming to the set budget and trying to make it work daily.

Issues Which Can Affect Your Campaigns

As a marketer, you can improve your skills to the point that each campaign you build reaches the highest quality, with a perfect target audience, messaging, and timing. Unfortunately, even the best prepaid campaign can fail miserably and the worst part—it might not even be your fault. Issues with a website or app, forms not working, carts not working, a server crash, a URL was changed or replaced but kept in the ads, and many more factors which are out of your control can have an effect on your campaigns.

Imagine running a campaign for $10,000 a day and paying for each click, only to find out a few days later that the LP was down, or had issues such as a button not working. As a result, you were sending users to a page where it was either impossible or very difficult for them to convert. While that might sound unlikely, it can and does happen often. If you are lucky, the cart or form will not work at all, in which case you can figure out there is a problem once you see sales or leads have dropped to zero.

As a digital marketer, it is not enough to be the chef who only barks orders; you need to cook, wait, and run the rest of the home front. When a large-scale campaign is up and running, test every aspect of the campaign before you launch, and be prepared to test every day while the campaign is live.

If you are sending customers to a cart, try buying something yourself. If you send them to a form, fill it out and make sure it's received. Make sure the LP comes up and test the links you set in your ads to make sure the experience is seamless for your potential clients. Additionally, when possible, make sure your codes, especially conversion codes, are up and working properly. Some advertising platforms offer tools to test; for example, Google has Tag Assistant, Facebook has Pixel Helper, and Twitter has Pixel Helper.

A missing or broken conversion code can harm your campaigns on a few levels. For starters, it won't count conversions, you won't know which campaigns worked, and you won't be able to optimize. If you run target CPA bidding campaigns, which are campaigns that are set to self-optimize based on a conversion cost you set, lack of tracking can mean these campaigns go haywire trying to find sales. It will throw off the algorithm and can take a few weeks to fix once the code is working again.

Remarketing: A Chance to Shed Light on Your Product

Remarketing, or retargeting as some call it, is when you place a pixel on your site that in turn places a cookie on the browser of anyone who visits your site. This enables targeting these visitors with ads about your product when they visit other sites containing ads from the pixel providers platform. For example, if you use an AdWords remarketing code on your site, you will be able to target any visitor who visits other sites containing AdSense banners.

While this is a widely used practice and chances are you've heard of remarketing before, how you set it up can make all the difference between a long term successful campaign or one where you may get sales, but do more harm than good. Remarketing should act as a reminder or enlightener to people who may have visited but not converted. The general reasons why someone wouldn't purchase your product right away include:

- **Not interested:** As much as you hate to admit it, some people simply are not interested in your product, no matter how amazing or good you think it is.

- **Interested but too busy at the moment:** Life gets busy, sometimes we see things we are interested in and say, "I'll do it later." That's why some of us put off our taxes until the last minute or find out we don't have matching socks when we're late for work.

- **Interested but requires more research:** The first thought of this person is, "Wow great product." The person's second train of thought is, "I wonder if there is anything similar on the market? Can this really work? Who is behind this product? Can I trust them?"

- **Interested but wants to shop around:** This is the bargain shopper who likes the product but think they might find it at Walmart or somewhere else cheaper.

- **Interested but wrong timing:** Either for them or for your product (presale, season, etc.,) Wrong timing can mean wrong from a personal level such as, love it but can't afford it at the moment, or the product just doesn't make sense for them right now. For example, a great pair of Sunglasses, but it's winter now, so I'll wait till summer and see if they are still in fashion.

- **Interested but got distracted:** "Wow look at this I want one of these, oh wait my phone is ringing, oh I'm late for a meeting..."

When you run a remarketing campaign, you should take all these scenarios and others you can think of into account. The idea is not to simply bombard users with your ads until they hopefully buy your product. Instead, your campaigns should bring value or shed new light on the product. Make sure it's engaging and tells a story they may have missed on your site. After all, if a customer didn't purchase the first time they visited your site, it's likely due to one of the reasons listed above, or you simply did not communicate well with that visitor. Remarketing gives you that extra chance to get it right.

A few things to make sure of:

- Add the list of "purchasers" as an exemption rule to all your remarketing lists. It's one thing to advertise to those who didn't buy, but why annoy or waste impressions on those who did. The list of purchasers can be used in other ways, for example, when trying to upsell or offer something to those who already purchased, such as offering a discount on the second item. By adding the purchasers list as an exclusion, you also ensure that any visitors that take action due to your remarketing or other campaigns will automatically be removed from your targeting.

- Limit your lists by timeline: seven days, fourteen days, and thirty days, and exclude the previous lists from the other lists. For example, the fourteen days list should exclude seven days and the thirty days list should exclude seven and fourteen days. This will enable you to provide different ad copy and styles for people in various stages of the buying cycle. Additionally, you don't want your ads to get stale. By splitting up the lists by timeline and adding different copy to each list, your remarketed visitors will be taken on a journey and get to see new sides of your product.

- If you have multiple items, you can use dynamic remarketing which will show your visitors ads with the items they were interested in.

- Once your campaigns have been live for at least a month, so you have sufficient data, look at the placement data and see where conversions are actually coming from. This can give you insight into specific sites your target audience visits and enable you to create new campaigns targeting these placements. You can then also create new remarketing campaigns targeting only visits of those placements to be more competitive on those sites and have more control.

- Create remarketing campaigns targeting specific sites that are high value to you. Remarketing generally costs less per click than traditional marketing, and also gets precedence on most websites, as the likelihood of a click on a remarketing ad is higher than on a traditional placement ad. This means that the advertising platform would rather make 1$ CPC ten times than a $3 CPC twice. Additionally, by retargeting your audience on a specific site such as the NYT, you improve the brand perception for those visitors and thus improve your brand effect.

- Frequency capping is marketing's best friend. Nothing is worse than bombarding your audience with ads, even if you do it timeline based. The last thing you want is for your audience to feel spammed, as this may turn off your prospective customers. Limit the frequency your ads are shown.

- Filter your lists to only target people who spent a certain amount of time on your site. The longer a person remains on your site, the chances are greater that they were actually interested. This is especially beneficial when running broad targeting, as it helps weed out the people who were not really interested to learn more about your product.

- In most cases it makes sense to send someone who clicks on a remarketing banner to a landing page created just for them highlighting all the benefits they may have missed and when possible, providing them with a special offer. Sending them back to the same landing page they originally ignored may work, but likely won't.

There is a clear benefit to running remarketing, but it's crucial to do it with tact, and as a way to prime customers, not bombard them.

Part 8:
Social Media as Part of The Online Strategy

Overview

Social media is an integral part of any online marketing strategy. However, that doesn't mean any social media. Social media comes in all sorts of forms and platforms: Facebook, Twitter, LinkedIn, Pinterest, and Instagram are probably the best known, but there are hundreds of platforms. What is clear about social media is that, aside from Facebook, which is a general social media platform, they are, for the most part, either topic based or function based. What I mean is that they are either geared around a particular topic or how you use them; for example, LinkedIn is a professional network; Twitter is based on how you interact (Tweets); Instagram is based on image creation, and Pinterest is based on image pins and creating personal boards.

Running a social media presence is its own strategy, but when combined with your online strategy, the same rules apply. You need to focus on the social platform with the best type of use or topic to reach your target audience while taking into account the mindset of people using these platforms. With most social platforms posting content and updates, having many likes and followers is for the most part necessary for the company brand, but does less to contribute to the sales funnel. So the online strategy will account for the paid portion of these social networks. In the past few years social networks, especially Facebook, have limited the organic exposure posts receive.

The reason given for this is that there are so many posts created and so many posts that any individual can receive based on their network and likes, that a method is needed to limit the amount of content to content that is more relevant to each user. Content from your friends will usually reach you without a filter, as it's highly relevant to you. So the real fight for your Facebook newsfeed is not between your friends, but between pages you liked and paid content.

How does Facebook do this? They use CTR as a promotion trigger. This means that the better the initial CTR of a post, the greater the chance of it outperforming its rivals. Why CTR? Simple. If people like your content and click on it, Facebook sees it as highly relevant to the audience. The algorithm is set to open each post by triggers. For example, let's say you posted to your wall, and your post started reaching your page fans, and from the first viewers you get a 1% CTR, chances are your post will stop delivering. However, if those first viewers get a 10% CTR the algorithm will open it, so that your post will reach more of your audience until the CTR starts to drop too low at which point it will stop serving.

A common practice that was used by many marketers is buying likes. These were usually from "Like Farms" with fake users liking your page. So, rather than spending thousands of dollars acquiring a real audience, you could opt to buy the same number of users for a few dollars. This was most popular at a time when how many Likes you had on your page was measured and perceived as a sign of your pages/company's popularity and authenticity. The main issues with this, however, is that while it gives your page a high like count, the quality of likes will probably be extremely poor. It increases the cost of reaching your own true page likers. For example, let's say you have 1,000 real page likes, but then bought 50,000 fake likes. If you were to run an ad to try and influence your true fans those who organically liked your page, you would have to spend a lot of money to reach all 51,000 fans, just to get to your original 1,000. Additionally, going back to the CTR for organic posts, you can just imagine how this would affect your CTR, even if you had the most engaging post in the world. Luckily, this is a less common practice these days, as more and more marketers understand the value of a real audience and the harm of a fake one. That said, even with a quality audience, getting organic posts widely spread is very difficult unless you are a super brand, or have extremely interesting content for your viewers. For this reason, most of social has turned to paid. It not only lets you target your own Facebook page fans but also to reach new audiences. A well-balanced social strategy blends highly engaging organic posts with highly relevant paid social ads.

Often I am asked how many posts should be created each day, week, or month, and my answer is always the same: If you don't have a post that will bring value or interest to your audience, don't post it. Posting content just for the sake of posting takes away from your social media manager's time. Posting content just for the sake of posting also provides those who see it with zero or even negative value and will not reach much of your audience anyway. The same should apply to paid content; there is no reason to force your audience to view content they wouldn't want to see organically.

Influencer Marketing and How to Influence Influencers

Influencer marketing is all the rage at the moment. The idea of paying individuals who have a large social following to promote your product is not new. Advertisers have been using celebrities for their campaigns for decades. The real shift is not in the concept of using influencers but in the categorization of who an influencer is. With the continued growth of social media, more and more individuals have taken the spotlight without the need for a big contract or sophisticated tools. All you need to become an influencer is the will to expose yourself on social networks along with some talent, and you can grow your own fan base.

Every field has its audience, so, for example, people such as Jenna Marbles, on YouTube, make a career from entertaining us with silly videos about life's intricacies, to vloggers who show us the latest iPad features, or how to pass level eight of our favorite game. While many influencers are self-proclaimed, larger companies are catching on quickly and adapting.

LinkedIn, for example, marks high profile accounts as "INfluencers." These accounts can then be followed, and LinkedIn will suggest accounts to you to follow based on your profession and groups. Additionally, they opened up LinkedIn personal posts so that anyone could create articles and share them through their LinkedIn account. New startups, such as live streamer "You Now," are emerging to enable influencers to reach their audiences in new ways.

Marketers today can choose influencers to market their products based on the influencer's field, their audience, and general product fit. Sites like HYPR, Tailify, Influicity, and Famebit make it easy to sift through hundreds of influencers to find your match and make a deal. Prices are usually based on the influencer's reach, and the work needed. In some cases, a single Facebook post or Tweet can cost thousands of dollars. While that may sound expensive, consider that celebrities can take hundreds of thousands, to millions for similar services. Thus, this is not always a bad alternative. Sure, you won't have the same effect or reach as Beyoncé behind your brand, but the right influencer and target audience can help make those needed ripples.

But what if you don't have millions, hundreds of thousands, or even thousands of dollars?

The one thing most of us overlook when it comes to influencers and celebrities is that they are just like us. Yes, they get paid to say they like some products, but just like all of us, they have their favorite drinks, jeans, apps, and even toothpaste. More often than not, they are happy to give props and share what they like without compensation.

In today's digital world, marketers should not only plan strategies and campaigns to reach potential buyers, but should also plan and execute marketing campaigns to reach celebrities, influencers, media professionals, and even potential business partners and investors.

How can this be achieved? Start by mapping out your influencers based on your target audiences and see how these influencers interact with them. Make sure the types of influencers you place on your list are the ones who would best convey your products. Next, research your influencers. See where they are most active and ascertain if an interaction by them on their leading go-to social platform would fit the mindset you are looking for.

This step may require some time and effort, but you want to ensure the paid effort you put into marketing has the highest chances to yield the desired results. Once you have a list of influencers and have researched them, it's time to match each influencer with the best possible messaging to get their attention and choose the platform on which you will reach out to them.

Some influencers can be easily reached. For example, if the company you are marketing has a new product release and you want to achieve PR you could post the news to your company's LinkedIn page. Better yet, link it to a publication's coverage of it, and promote your post on LinkedIn targeting users by titles, such as "Editor" or "Blogger/ Vlogger." If you want to reach celebrities, all you need to do is have a look at a standard "Map to the stars," and you can target their homes by zip code or radius. Then use either AdWords or Facebook ads so that anyone in that household will see them.

You can also take the approach of simply sending them your product in hopes of them using it and giving you that coveted shout out. Some products might even be helpful for an influencer. For example, if you sell filming equipment, audio equipment or even have a product that could help the influencer grow their own brand, they will likely be happy to receive it.

Influencers have two main goals: they want to make money doing what they love, and they want to grow their audience, which in turn leads to more income.

Some approaches may be easier and more fruitful than others. With these campaigns, as with any online campaign, it's all about patience, optimization, and trying new things. The rise of influencers is exciting and has yielded an entirely new industry, giving more people the power to express themselves, and, well, influence audiences. With the right strategy, you can get influencers and celebrities to hear about your product and become customers, and even feature your products.

You can get media to write about your products, and give potential business partners and investors the illusion that your company is much stronger and bigger than it is.

No matter our status, we are all people. We all purchase products, liking some and disliking others. Marketers market to people, to other marketers, and they can definitely influence the influencers.

Dark Social and Why It Matters

"Dark Social" is a concept you may have heard of. It refers to social interactions that are hidden from the marketer's eyes. For example, emails people write to each other, posts on friends' walls, or private messaging; in other words, dark social is similar to word of mouth, which is generally hard to assess. Whenever there is a discussion about your product, either positive or negative, you can be assured there is a wider dark social effect taking place.

Not everyone who is unhappy or even thrilled with your product will run to your webpage to let you know about it. For every client who complains or requests a feature, there are tens or even hundreds like them who simply keep it to themselves or look for your competitors. While you can't see people's private messages or emails, there are other ways to get an idea of what your market is saying about you, and not to you.

I often join various groups and discussions that my target audience is likely to be a part of. By doing this, I gain insight into their general interests which can help me formulate messaging. I also tap into group discussions about the product, that while not being completely personal, allow me to have a similar interaction with users. Frustrated customers tend to let their frustration be heard. It's all about understanding where that frustration is likely to be unleashed.

If you are a software company, joining discussions on Quora for example, or searching your own product, is a great way to see what your product is missing, what is unclear to users, or what frustrates your customers. Naturally, dark social does not have to be negative. Positive feedback and compliments can also go a long way to understanding what your customers think you are doing right, which can help you retain and expand on those factors. Whether positive or negative, it is important to gather as many insights as possible before jumping to conclusions based on a few people's opinions.

Part 9:
Content Marketing

Overview

Content comes in all shapes and sizes, from simple social posts to blog posts, white papers, and even eBooks like this one. When it comes to content marketing, the content needs to be tailored to its audience. For example, if your audience is used to getting large amounts of information before making a decision such as CTOs who are looking for a new tech system, a white paper might be more useful for them to make a decision.

If your audience is marketers, you may want to opt for blog posts which provide a quick and visual understanding of the product. And if you are selling to the masses, your content may be a YouTube video or a social post. In some cases, multiple content methods could work for a single target, but how that content is presented will make or break the content strategies success.

One approach, which I particularly like, is using your content strategy to gain awareness for your product or service but also tell a story. This brings your audience into your company's inner workings and takes them on a journey.

When customers feel like they are part of your world they will be more interested and invested in what you have to offer. It can be as simple as posting to your social network not just with what you want them to do, but with a more personal touch. Show them what you are up to, how your product is progressing, introduce them to your team, tell them a touching story about how the company got where it is, or something that happened to an employee. And when writing more professional content such as white paper, show why you are an authority on the subject.

Content marketing is not really about content; it's about reaching your audience on a personal level and making them part of your story.

Authorship: Lead to Succeed

Becoming an authority is one of the highest goals a company or individual can strive for. It's one thing to be good at or known for something, but once people look to your company for answers and expertise, your company becomes a real opinion shaper. A brand then has *prestige*. It is trusted and conceived to be of the highest quality.

Google used authorship as a way to connect content creators to their online publications and to help them get notability. It also meant that publishers with high authority would help sites with their content rank higher, but the terms have evolved to present a state of acceptance of a company as an opinion leader.

If you want to buy sports shoes, you would probably look at Nike, Reebok, and Adidas. Even if other companies provide the same quality shoe for less, you believe you can trust these brands as authorities in the shoe industry. Getting to that status, however, takes time. You need to actively present authorship to your customers, similar to a doctor who hangs their degrees on the wall of their practice. Authorship is why VPs join panels and give speeches. Building authorship starts with every employee and spreads out to various channels of social media, PR, and content marketing.

Let's look at Google, for example. They are known for many groundbreaking products. But more than that, they are known for employing the best minds. Their leadership encourages employees to grow. They host and join events on an ongoing basis, not only to promote their products but also to demonstrate they are an industry leader. They have taken authorship and turned it into mentorship, not only by being the trusted authority to reach out to but also by embracing companies and mentoring them on how to best utilize their products.

Authorship can also be helped by campaign messaging. When you run online campaigns, your ads do more than just reach people and build awareness; they are very much a part of your branding. How they represent your company can make a huge difference to the company's authorship.

How will you know that you have achieved authorship? Aside from the increase in organic customers and that warm feeling inside, you will most likely notice bloggers and writers using your company as an example of accomplishment and quoting your management and employees. Your social mentions will rise, and you will increasingly be asked to join panels and speak at events. In other words, your company will reach a state of respect from both customers and peers.

Don't Wait For PR, Create It

Having respectable publications within your industry write about your company can help it build awareness, grow its audience, and gain trust. To get covered by publications, you need to check a few of their boxes. Your product or the new feature has to be interesting enough to write about, and more importantly, it has to interest their audience. You want to make sure that when publications do write about you, they write the correct information about your company, and show you in a positive light. Most companies will only ever get a handful of mentions unless they continually evolve, so make that handful count!

- Make sure your online assets are clear and possess the message you want to be featured. Be clear about the benefits people receive from your service or product.

- Make sure what sets you apart is clear and easy to find. Does the company hold a patent and is it unique?

- While your content is mainly for your customers, add elements to help prospective media build a story as well.

- Make sure to add clearly visible and easy to find contact information for the media to connect with your PR department. Nothing is worse than a journalist's email getting into the wrong hands or into the general email pool. After all, you might be a hot topic today, but tomorrow you could be old news.

- Get your social sites right. Even if you are not a big believer in social networks, make no mistake, they are a big part of any journalist's research. The low activity could give an impression of weakness in your industry and irrelevant content can show desperation or lack of a voice. Positive or negative feedback on your social networks and how you react to them are also very important factors. Make sure you don't have too many social skeletons in your online closet.

- Make sure your company is on LinkedIn, and that all associated accounts look legit. Like it or not, every respectable company is on LinkedIn.

- Once you have dotted all your I's and crossed all your T's, you are ready to present your company to the world. To get featured, you first need to get noticed. It's not enough to just exist, but you must be active to get attention.

- Follow editors, bloggers, and publications on Twitter. Some may follow you back, and others may find you interesting enough to look up. So be sure to add your website to your profile. While they may not write about you right away, your posts now have a chance of reaching them. Post often, and follow new accounts daily.

- Join LinkedIn groups and be active. The groups you join should be related to your industry, not just to your direct product or service.

- Join discovery networks, such as Product Hunt.

- Create ads on LinkedIn and Facebook targeting media professionals by groups or title, but keep your posts informational. They should look like they are aimed at your customers and just happen to cross paths with the media. You want the journalist/blogger to feel like they discovered you, not the other way around.

Email Marketing

Email has been around forever. Ok maybe not forever, it's been around since 1971 when Ray Tomlinson sent himself a test email at Cambridge. The point is it has survived as a valid communication tool, which is still one of the most widely used tools for both private and business communications.

These days when you want to reach out to a friend, you will most likely text them unless you have a lot to say or want to send a long email to all your friends. In the business world, however, texting is reserved for those you have already built a relationship with. You wouldn't text a potential customer or partner before making an initial connection.

Email is also where most people prefer to get their communication from companies. When given a choice to get your bills, newsletters, and promotions via email or text, most will prefer email as it's less invasive. We also use email as a way to communicate with companies as it gives us a way to save the correspondence in case of need and easily find it later.

As much as we all love email and it is integrated into our daily lives, it's also another source of spam, in fact, that's where spam got its online start. And no one likes spam. Because of the amount of spam, and companies buying lists of emails, and of course the malware and viruses that are spread via email, people are cautious when opening emails. Companies like Google have also created filters within Gmail for spam, so there is an algorithm that flags emails as spam if it diagnoses the email as such. The triggers for a possible spam can come from the email's content, the URL it came from, the number of emails which were sent, and other such factors.

As marketers, it's important to incorporate email into the sales funnel, but for your emails to be successful and to reach your audience and get favorable results, you need to take several factors into account.

There are different types of emails your customers should be receiving. These include:

Transactional Emails

Transactional emails include automated emails based on an action taken by the customer. For example, if the customer signed up for a newsletter, a transactional email would be one welcoming them to the newsletter and acknowledging that they signed up. If an item was purchased, then the customer would receive an email confirmation and even an invoice or receipt.

It's important to treat these emails with the respect they deserve. While they are simple emails which confirm an action taken, they are a touch point with your customers. The way the email looks and your branding on it, even the messaging, all play to your customers' perceptions. Additionally, while only a transactional email, these can also be used to deliver additional information or value to your customers. For example, an email may include the following message, "Thank you for signing up to our newsletter, we appreciate your interest in our business, here's a free coupon to use on your next order."

Newsletter Sign Ups

Then there are newsletter sign ups; these are emails sent to people who actively want to get updates from you. As a best practice and depending on your business, you should try and gain an understanding of what type of updates these people are interested in; this can be part of the signup process. When people did sign up for your newsletter, by doing so, they created a bond of trust with you, meaning they trust you to send them emails, that trust can be easily broken with swamps of emails pushing product. A person who signed up for your newsletter is either already a customer or is interested in your product already. Make your newsletter about value and insight into your product and business, not an endless sales pitch.

Promotional Emails

Finally, there are promotional emails, and these are the ones that are aimed at increasing sales or sign ups. These are also the emails that are most likely to end up in a spam box or be ignored. They can also lead your audience to unsubscribe from a mailing list if they feel pestered.

When sending a promotional email, it's important first to examine your mailing list, remove any customers who have previously complained about your product/service, and filter for people who are more likely to be interested in this particular offer. Don't treat all your email lists as one unit. Just as with your newsletter, send promotions only if they truly have value, and don't overdo it. From a technical standpoint, large lists should be split up and sent out slowly. If you send out 100k emails all at once, you have a higher chance of being flagged as spam, especially if you have not previously sent bulk emails from that URL.

Some people believe that timing your email isn't as important as it would be with social media, but it is still a factor to consider. Sending an email at night, for example, might mean your customer gets it when they are going over many emails first thing in the morning. Many workers start their day responding to emails and getting them out of the way. For this reason, an email sent mid-day might work better than an email sent in the middle of the night or early morning. This naturally needs to be tested and will differ depending on the audience.

Your title messaging is the single most important feature of your email. It doesn't matter how well designed or how great an offer you present in your email if people don't open it. Your messaging doesn't need to be fancy or complicated; it needs to be clear. When seeing the email, a person should be able to understand clearly who it's from and what you are offering. There are many psychological tactics which can be used to evoke mystery or excitement, but the general rule I have found is that the user needs to have a good enough trigger to want to see what's inside.

As with any campaign, analyzing results is key to success. You want to look at the full effect of your email marketing, not only the successes. Your emails could very well have a positive effect, but they can also have a negative one which could even make your email more harmful than productive. Let's look at an example.

A few years ago, I joined Wix to build websites and landing pages on my own. It's a fairly simple tool, and I find it useful for small businesses. When I just started out with Wix, I received an email about six months after signup and the title read something like "50% OFF all renewals for a limited time".

Considering that I was a customer and would have to renew some of my websites, this looked like a great deal, and so I opened the email and rushed to renew all my sites. However, over the years I kept getting the same offer in different emails. The copy had slightly changed, the graphics changed, but the offer was still the same 50% off.

Don't get me wrong; it's still a good offer. However, now instead of rushing to open the email, I had no reason to do so. I already knew what it's about, and instead of thinking this is a great deal, it got me thinking that buying at full price was silly, since 50% off is offered all year round. It also lowered Wix's conceptual value for me to the point where I now see the full price as outrageous.

The main takeaway is to constantly evaluate the full effect your emails may have on your customers. For every customer you turned on to our product, you may also be turning people away.

Part 10:
Mobile App Marketing

Overview

Mobile app marketing is a unique challenge, as it presents marketers with multiple obstacles to overcome. Unlike physical products or services which usually have their own website and controlled environments, with apps, the sale takes place in a third-party environment (the App/Play store). This gives each app marketer limited options in terms of branding and also creates a leveled playing field where all try to rank at the top.

There are many theories about what makes an app rise in the charts, but the only theory that I know of to be proven is the number of installs the app gets. The more daily installs, the higher the app will rank. Getting those installs in a sustainable manner is what it's all about. Why rank high? The first reason is the exposure you get from people who are visiting the store looking for new apps to try. The higher you rank, the more truly organic installs you will get. The second reason ranking high is important is that it sheds light on your app in other ways such as PR and authorship. In other words, "It's good to be King."

Additionally, unlike some products where return customers are not expected on a daily or weekly basis, with apps, especially free apps, return usage is crucial for the app's survival. In most cases, you have seven days to hook a user and 30 days to retain a user. This means if you don't manage to impress users within seven days of them installing, they will most likely leave never to return. If you don't manage to make the app part of their daily routine within 30 days, the same will apply.

The unfortunate truth is that most people who visit a store won't download the app, and of those who do, most won't use it more than once. A standard phone, for example, an iPhone, has 24 apps it can show on page 1 of the phone's home screen. The apps on page 1 are usually the apps that a person uses the most. Apps on other pages are usually used only once in a while, or go to what is rightfully called the app's "graveyard." Once an app is in someone's graveyard, it's hard for it to be resurrected.

For your app strategy to be successful, you will have to fight this battle on all fronts. You will need to bring your storefront to its best possible presentation of your app with enticing graphics and outstanding messaging. You will also need to acquire quality users who will not only install, but actually want to use your app. And finally, you will have to do all that's in your power to provide these users with an exceptional experience so that they keep coming back. There are many tools and strategies for retention. However, a well-produced product is usually the key factor.

Approach Mobile App Marketing from the Upside Down

On average, 90 percent of startups will not succeed. If your startup is an app it's even more challenging. You are not only fighting for your place amongst thousands, but also for the sought after real-estate we each have in our pockets. While most people may have over 100 apps on their phone, only some of those apps will be on their main screen, and of the apps on the home screen, only some of those apps will be regularly used.

Why do most companies create an app in the first place? It's usually a financial decision. However, businesses can get obsessed with the vision of the product itself, and leave the financial aspects for later. This can lead them down the wrong path before they even get started. While the app idea is essential, how you take your app to market and your monetization plan will ultimately determine its success.

Monetization has its own set of rules, and its own value for each country where your ads are shown, generally presented in CPM (1 thousand views). For example, if your ads are shown in Saudi Arabia they may be worth $1 CPM, and if they are shown in the U.S. they may be worth $3 CPM. But that worth also comes at a price. For example, getting an install in Saudi Arabia might cost you $0.10 CPI (cost per install), whereas getting an install in the U.S. may cost you $2 CPI.

In order to make the best decision for your app's marketing strategy, you need to turn things upside down. This means, start by understanding where the market is, not which market is more valuable based on common misconceptions. If you are in the midst of planning your app and are wondering how to get it to market, first aim to understand which markets make the most sense financially, not emotionally or based on perception. Then plan and make your product ready for those markets.

Once you have a list of countries where your app may work, and you understand your reach potential, get estimations of the CPI for that country and understand the monetization CPM for that country. You may be surprised to learn that some countries pay high CPMs (even close to U.S.), but have much lower CPIs. In other words, cheaper traffic to buy with higher overall margins, when comparing CPM to the added buying power.

Other considerations, which make this a more compelling approach, is the app ranking value. As previously explained, apps are ranked in each country and category mainly by the number of daily installs they receive. Apps which rank higher, get more exposure and in turn more organic, non-paid installs. Therefore, the more installs you can afford to buy, the higher you will rank the more organic (free) installs you will get. These are installs which didn't cost you money but will still make you money from your monetization.

Understanding where your most valuable audience is located is only part of the equation. We all have apps we love and can't get enough of. Although we also have apps we used to love and forgot about or ones that just didn't make it through the first audition. For an app to make it into our list of used apps, it must provide value and be on our minds. But more importantly, it needs to become part of our daily or weekly routine.

There are many ways app developers can go about engaging their users in that first month. These may include: push notifications, emails, retargeting campaigns, and other promotions. For an app to thrive, it's not enough to purchase users; your app will have to grow organically. For this to happen, you must build the app for growth. You may embed elements in the app that either prompt the user to invite their friends and community or share it with them.

For an app to dramatically improve its chances for success, acquisition and retention should be built into the app's core. For example, making it easy to invite friends and also promoting friend invites, promoting content sharing and ensuring those shares link back to your app. Promoting should not include simply having the option available, but actually making it compelling and suggestive to do so.

When you create a product, people will see value in it. If you offer it to the right audience and make it easy, fun, and suggest people invite their friends and share their experience, every dollar you place into acquiring them becomes a multiplier, as they will invite friends who will join and invite their friends and share content and so on. What separates successful apps from others are not only getting new users but also understanding how to leverage their app into a growth machine.

Gamification: Making A Play for Growth

Gamification is another way to leverage growth. While we may not like to admit it, deep down we are all still children who want to play and be entertained. Companies who embrace this idea can create a world within their product for their users. Waze, the traffic avoidance app that was acquired by Google is a great example of gamification.

The concept of Waze is brilliant and straightforward. Each driver using the app acts as a beacon. When the algorithm notices a cluster of users in the same spot and moving at a slow pace, it assumes there is a traffic jam when there is no traffic light in the vicinity. Additionally, each user can report obstacles in the way, such as a car stopped on the shoulder, police, and various other warnings.

Each Waze user gets an icon when they join, and points every time they help and submit information. Users can also actively edit the map. Additionally, as you use the app more, and help other drivers, you get new funny rank upgrades, and your reports get a greater influence. I, for example, am currently a knight. You can also choose an icon to go with your mood, and editors have exclusive icons such as a robot or T-rex. Also, you gain points by adding friends to Waze, which is a great way for them to expand organic growth. Waze aims not to be simply a traffic avoidance app, but a driver's social activism network, where people help people get around and enjoy doing so.

While there is no monetary benefit yet to being a high level or contributing (which may change as they introduced Carpool which is a platform where people can get paid for driving others going to the same destination), people love the vibe and the social aspect.

Gamification is not for every business, and it has to be done well to work. But it can be a great tool for boosting user engagement and retention.

ASO (App Store Optimization)

ASO (App Store Optimization) is similar in concept to SEO in that you want to improve how your app shows up both in search engine results and in the app/play stores themselves. With ASO, however, writing (keyword) space is limited as you only have your storefront. The most important text elements are your title and the short description. The title helps people find your product and holds valuable keywords.

The short description is your main sales pitch, and it's the first bit of information after your title that users get to see. Treat it as you would a site meta description, meaning it should explain your app and sell it all at once. The long description is also very important, but less so than the short description.

Other elements that can help with ASO are your app's rating, generally ranging from 1-5. It's an indication for visitors and the store publisher of the quality of your app. Apps with good ratings will get more installs and have a better chance of being featured. Having a built in rating system and actively asking your users to rate your app can go a long way. You would, however, want to segment your users and approach only those likely to give you a good rating.

Improving your place in search results is only part of the equation. Your app icon is the single most important asset you have to draw people to your app, as it's the only element that is clearly visible to people visiting the app stores. For that reason, you should try and have one that stands out from the other apps in your category. The icon should clearly portray what your app is about and set the expectations.

The app market is a global space. For that reason, having your app in a single language or poorly translated language is a sure way to limit your reach. Localize your app as you would a website, and don't rely on automated translations. Also have your store's texts and visuals professionally translated. Whenever possible, you should also have your app content translated so that individuals can download an app in their native language.

As with SEO, having articles and social pages which link to your store will help get more traffic to your stores. However, unlike with websites, I have yet to see any evidence that having links to your store improves its ranking in any way. While ASO might sound like a complex practice, you shouldn't get overwhelmed by it. The main take away is to understand that all the elements your store is comprised of matter and need to be well thought through and designed, as well as evaluated and tested on a regular basis.

PART 11:

AIMING FOR GROWTH

Overview

"**Growth hacking** is a process of rapid experimentation across marketing channels and product development to identify the most effective, efficient ways to grow a business. **Growth hacking** refers to a set of both conventional and unconventional marketing experiments that lead to **growth** of a business." (Wikipedia)

Growth hacking is a term which was coined by Sean Ellis. Many marketers tend to look forward with their growth efforts, looking for the next best way to market. While it's good to have that kind of spirit and to try various methods to achieve growth, this can also lead to neglecting or not paying attention to what you already have.

Many companies take steps to try and achieve growth, but while they may be stepping forward, they are not stepping up. Growth hacking, at its core, is looking first at your product, as well as marketing assets, and finding ways to tweak or enhance them for improved organic growth results. For example, learning how people find your product, what they search for, how they use it, why they use it, and then using that data to expand those areas. This differs than A/B testing, where you are testing certain features such as a color or image, or even a new website. Like many aspects of marketing, growth hacking begins with research and evaluation and then uses those findings to establish a strategy.

Before you tackle growth hacking, you must first understand how growth is achieved. This can differ for each product or service, but for all, it starts with understanding which doors are already open and how your customers behave. A good example would be a company selling a variety of products online. When looking into which products sell the most, and why, the company can come to many conclusions such as how to do the same for other products, or shift focus to the best performing if they find good reason.

For example, you may notice that all the best-selling products are in a particular location on the site, or they fall within the same price range. Maybe they fall into a specific category of products or are products promoted with a similar sales pitch. Understanding what factors are causing these products to sell better can assist you to either improve the sales of those products or to take that information and use it to promote the other products.

Many marketers look at metrics such as bounce rate, or time on site, time spent on a certain page, and other measurements to understand how well their website is performing. But they don't narrow down their view to the visitors, the ones who matter and actually buy. Customers can come to a site in many different ways, from finding it randomly, to word of mouth, articles, and of course paid campaigns. But most of those people are window shoppers.

Thus, evaluating how they interact with your website alongside your actual buyers will give you an extremely distorted view of your website's performance. You can narrow your view to purchasers only, and learn how they arrived at your site, how much time they spend there, and even how they interact socially with your products. You can then tweak the site to cater to them. You can make the products they like easiest to find, while removing clutter, so your site is optimized for completing a purchase, but also for growth.

Sharing is probably the best compliment a customer can give, and it's one of the only social actions that promotes direct growth. Learn how your customers prefer to share. You can highlight the social buttons most used by your shoppers. For example, let's say you have a B2B product and people who buy on your site like sharing it on LinkedIn. Or maybe you have a visual product like jewelry, and promoting sharing on Instagram is the way to go. By understanding your real value to customers and catering to them, you will improve not only your sales but also your organic growth.

Additionally, while many tweaks improve sales on a site, they don't necessarily promote direct growth. After all, growth is about getting more customers. Just like a real store, the better the experience you give your customers, the more they will return and at the same time spread the word to other potential customers.

Are we really going to ignore all those "window shoppers?" Of course not, because every website visitor is either a potential buyer who might simply be in a preliminary buyer's cycle stage or a potential brand ambassador. The idea is not to ignore any visitor. They are all valuable, but your goal should be to understand how to best cater to them individually. Some people don't know how to sift through a site and find what they need or understand fast enough to make a decision. By tweaking the site towards buyers, you are only making it easier for everyone else.

Is that all there is to growth hacking? The truth is that every marketer sees growth hacking differently. Some, such as myself, view growth hacking as a process of learning and tweaking your assets to get the full potential and generate quality growth. Others see it as using any means possible to generate growth, which could be anything from tricking customers into taking actions they wouldn't have naturally or putting them through a process that forces growth. Whichever road you choose, it's important to keep the quality of customers and your brand in mind.

To sum it all up, if you want to achieve real growth, start by actually understanding who your customers are. Create categories such as age groups, genders, and interests. Research how they prefer to learn about products: Do they like to read long articles or watch short videos? How do they take actions on a website? Do they have a preferred payment method? Do they have security concerns? Are there colors they prefer, or which fonts? Do they like offers, and which type of offer would be more impactful? And of course, how do they prefer to share, do they tweet, post to Facebook, or prefer more personal communications such as email and chat? By understanding these elements, you will be able to devise strategies which are growth-focused.

Turn Your Company into a Growth Machine

When it comes to growth, one commonly overlooked approach is that while not all employees are marketers, they can all have a part in your company's growth. Companies come in all shapes and sizes and have a diverse set of employees with various skill sets and responsibilities. While we would like to think of a company as a place where everyone works together to reach the same goal, in reality, each employee has their own job description, tasks, and responsibilities. And while each individual task helps the company reach its common goal, most employees in a company (unless they are on the same team) do not steer very far from their own duties.

But there is power in numbers; there is no question about that. If every person on earth would give $1 a day to a communal pot, we would probably be able to feed and shelter all the homeless or find cures for various illnesses. While getting $1 from each person on earth might not be a very sensible option, getting your own employees to support your company can be possible. I am not talking about your employees pitching in money, but rather their social resources and five minutes a day.

Here's an example, let's say your company sells software B2B, and you have 25 employees. If you are like most companies, one to two of those employees are your marketers, and they joined a combined 20 LinkedIn groups that they post on every time your company has news or something to share like a promotion. LinkedIn has a group-joining cap, so each individual can only join 50 groups. This helps them ensure people are actually active in the groups they join and limits spammers.

Now imagine if you were to create a sheet where each employee donates a portion of their 50 groups on LinkedIn. Let's say the average employee is willing to join ten groups that are purely for the companies benefit. The company now has a pool of 250 groups they can join. Next, they list all the related groups on LinkedIn and divide them up into categories and give each employee or a few of them groups from the same category.

Now each time there is either content created or received, the marketer's job is simply to send an email with that content to the relevant employees and ask them to post it to their ten groups.

By following this simple routine over time, your company will become its own content creation force. As it grows, so will your online presence, the ranking of your blog, and your company's overall authorship.

Crowdfunding: How to Fund Your Way to Success

Insidecoach is a Smart Soccer Ball that can track the power, speed, and trajectory of your kicks. Pulse-Play is a smart watch for tennis players, which helps them keep track of their game. It's like having a personal umpire on your wrist. AtmoTube is an air quality monitor that fits in your pocket and makes sure you know what quality of air you are breathing wherever you are. Ibubble is the world's first autonomous underwater drone.

What do they all have in common? They are all being made a reality thanks to crowdfunding. Each year, hundreds of products are being introduced on sites such as Kickstarter and Indiegogo, and some are making it big. But how simple is it really and should your product be crowd funded?

There are many types of crowdfunding, from charity to things like funding someone's dream of owning a lawn mower, to real innovative and useful products. Generally, the better performing campaigns are those that bring something new and innovative to the crowd. However, with so many campaigns going up each day, it's hard for your product to really stand out. One of the biggest and most impactful decisions is which platform to choose.

There are specified crowdfunding platforms for various types of funding. For example, for charity and personal funding, a popular one is GoFundMe. In reality, many of the "Charity" campaigns are mainly funded by family and friends, unless they get a huge PR push such as the "Greek Bailout Fund." If you want to be successful with crowdfunding, you need to choose your platform based on what you are funding for and understand who it is that visits these sites. Most crowdfunding visitors to the larger crowdfunding platforms, like Kickstarter and Indiegogo, are looking for cool new "toys." They want to be part of advancing technology and to be the first to own it as it comes out.

They are also the type of buyers who are willing to put up with not getting the product right away, and for the most part, they even tolerate delays. Additionally, even people who are not what you would typically consider an early adopter understand the mindset of crowdfunding, and act as early adopters on those platforms.

Here are some basic tips for the first time crowdfunder, or the failed crowdfunder who wants to give it another try:

- Choose your crowdfunding platform based on what you are asking for. If you are a charity, you will do better on a charity related crowdfunding platform then one aimed at tech.

- Invest in your product video. It doesn't have to be expensive, but it should showcase your product, tell your story, and explain your product. The same goes for images.

- Like any sales site, keep it short and to the point. No one wants to read a book about your product, as cool as you might think it is.

- Be authentic. Pitch something new, not just another product people can get elsewhere.

- Trust is key. Be transparent with your challenges and showcase your team. People want to know who is working on the project and what the chances are of actually getting the product.

- Your past is your future. When possible, show who you are. Emphasize your accomplishments, even from past ventures.

If you had a previously successful venture or even own one now, you will be trusted to deliver.

- Showcase it, don't pitch it! The crowdfunding audience is not one interested in a sales pitch. They are already in the mindset to buy, and they just need to fall in love.

- Your friends and family are your biggest allies, ask them to contribute and share your campaign as much as possible. No one wants to be the first to buy a product. Once you have some contributions, others will feel more comfortable to follow suit.

- Keep your perks reasonable and limit them. Too many extras will just scare people off. You also don't want to seem like all you are trying to do is find ways to get contributions.

- Buy traffic. Yes, I said it. Use paid advertising to get the right people to your page, just like you would for a regular store. While the audience on crowdfunding sites is open to new things, if you are selling tech ski boots, you need to make sure people who actually ski know about it. Sure, they might not be the crowdfunding audience, but if you target well, you can find your customers and let them know you exist. The drawback here is that users you bring in might want to see what else is available on the platform. But, if you target users who have intent, and are looking for products like yours or from the industry, you have a good chance of succeeding.

- Understand the costs and logistics involved in your product. Nothing is worse than reaching your goal only to realize you won't have enough to go to market, or worse, will lose on all of your backings. Finally, as with any business endeavor, your crowdfunding campaign should be planned ahead. You should have a schedule of what will be done on each day of the campaign to promote it, and PR should be lined up in advance. Every day you don't have contributors is a huge loss, so make them count.

Affiliate Marketing: Grow Your Own Army

While there are many ways to go about affiliate marketing, such as running your own affiliate program or joining an existing one, the concept is the same. Other websites place your ads on their websites and social networks, and you pay them a percentage of every sale. The big benefit with affiliate marketing is that the advertiser only pays when a sale takes place, or their desired action, like filling out a form. For the affiliate placing your ads on the site, it usually means an opportunity to get a larger sum than they would from other online ads.

So why doesn't everyone just do affiliate marketing? Well, for starters, in order for it to work well, the affiliate you work with has to have a very relevant placement for your ads. The website needs to cater to your target audience. If the affiliate does not see the type of profit they were after, they will drop you. Additionally, as with every type of advertising, you compete with others for that space. So, both sales of your product and return on your product must outperform the competing offers. This means that you don't only need to establish affiliates, but also keep them.

If you start your own affiliate network or go with an existing program such as Rakuten or CJ, the outreach and time needed to create and maintain your network will usually require a full-time affiliate manager. Pre-existing platforms bring with them the benefit of a network of affiliates already signed on to the program which you can pitch to, as well as the structure to manage it all. The drawbacks naturally include the costs and percentages you pay out to the network, which can be saved by starting your own network.

Generally speaking, affiliate marketing is great when you find the right partners and have the resources to maintain and grow it. If you don't, you can still start small and expand your resources as you grow. Affiliate marketing is overlooked by some marketing departments, as it's usually a long-term investment and won't give immediate results, which of course all depends on the partners you secure.

Going Global

For companies with an international presence, creating global campaigns is a no brainer. However, when creating these campaigns, it's important to factor in not only that your assets are translated, but also that your campaigns are setup correctly. One common mistake is to create campaigns that group multiple countries with the same language settings together, for example, a campaign that places the U.S., Canada, U.K., Australia, India, and South Africa together.

While this can save you time and make campaigns easier to manage, in reality, this type of grouping will limit the exposure each country receives because they will share the same budget. Additionally, as each location is in a different time zone, the bulk of the budget will go to the countries where people are awake first. For example, the U.K. might eat up all of the budget before the U.S. even starts searching.

By splitting up your campaigns by country, you ensure each country gets its own budget. It will give each one the maximum exposure while assisting you to optimize your decisions for each country with full transparency. If you must group countries, then do it by continent or proximity; U.S. and Canada can be one grouping, while the U.K., South Africa, and India can be in another.

When it comes to translation, it's best to use a translator who is a local in the targeted country. If the translator is not a local, or if they do not have a firm grasp of the country's vernacular, this may cause miscommunication of the product. Many countries have different dialects, slang, and sayings. While customers in those areas may understand what you mean, they will view the ads as amateurish, and that will affect their perception of your company.

Additionally, one of the greatest challenges I have encountered is companies who can handle selling globally, but simply decide to go after the U.S. market as a first step. The U.S. is known as a prime market for selling. However, other countries that are much cheaper to target, such as Australia, can be an overlooked goldmine. Australia has one of the highest percentages of online shoppers; the country also has one of the largest populations that has adopted PayPal as a main means of payment.

When a company launches a new product, especially tech products, online publications will generally write about it. If you have a good PR plan, many publications can pick it up. Once the main publishers write an article about a product, it's not long before other worldwide publications pick it up and write about it as well. Having your product available to those markets can help with your first boost of sales. Marketing globally can sometimes shift focus and help a company plan where to expand next.

The Importance of Localization

Localization is the process of taking your product or service, which was created in one geographic area and language and adapting it to others. It's more than simply translating your marketing materials into other languages. Instead, localization involves developing an understanding of another culture and appreciating what works for them. Some areas to keep in mind are colors you should use or avoid, or if translations should be to normative language or slang. What should you include on your images? Should you use images of locals, or can you stick with the materials you already have?

These are all areas to focus on when tackling localization. Imagine if you put in all the effort to target a specific country, and after spending millions on advertising, you find out that the colors are offensive in that country. That campaign may only give you minimal results, if any, due to that costly mistake. The best approach I have found is to hire a local to help you. It doesn't have to be a local marketer. In fact, in some cases, it's better not to. Instead, consider hiring someone from your target audience, and let their input assist in shaping your marketing efforts.

Sometimes localization is actually local. For example, if you go to certain tourist areas in countries like Thailand that rely mainly on tourists, you will find that many of the signs on stores, and advertisements are in English. Sometimes getting these wrong can be just as painful, although getting tourists to laugh may have the opposite effect.

How I Plan to Market This Book

If you are reading this book, which you clearly are, you may have found it in several ways. You could have found it by searching for online marketing books on Amazon or other publishers websites, or you may have seen an ad that I created and built campaigns to reach you and present you with a compelling enough messaging to read it. In other words, you have been marketed to read a book about marketing. Why am I sharing this with you? Well, I think it makes sense to bring everything you just read together and show you the kind of thinking that goes into a digital marketing strategy. And what better example than my own for this book?

How did I do this?

For starters, my assumed audience is marketers who have less experience with online or those looking to expand their knowledge, as well as business owners who are looking to improve their online presence. Additionally, I presume there are those simply interested in online marketing or marketing in general. These are very broad audiences, and I will initially be focusing on platforms where these audiences not only visit but actively look for content or even specifically eBooks.

As per messaging and marketing materials, I chose a title that both contains the information that book is about, so it will be easy to find and understand what it is with one glance, but also presents a whiff of mystery and a chance to look into the unknown. After all, who doesn't like a little mystery? Next, I researched the Amazon bookstore looking for other digital marketing books and designed a cover that would stand out from them while enhancing the title and mystery element. And what stands out more than a big Ninja pulling out a "digital sword"?

Next, and this is probably the most important part, I spent over a year collecting and establishing content which I find to have value. As previously stated, marketing can only do so much. A quality product is what really matters and what will make your customers become your ambassadors.

I then moved into the planning stage and researched the various options/platforms for marketing the book. I started by mapping out and creating social accounts, a Facebook page, a LinkedIn page, and Twitter account. On these accounts, I will periodically share insights from the book as well as promote my book directly. I also joined eBook groups on these platforms where I can post and promote it organically.

For paid outlets I looked at the various ad platforms to see what my options are. I found one issue which is that while I can promote my book on Amazon via third-party networks such as AdWords, Facebook, and LinkedIn, I probably won't be able to get tracking for it. This means that I will have to look at it as branding and create branding goals.

Amazon has its own advertising option for books, which I have signed on to and started testing campaign. To do this I placed the book as pre-order. I believe this will be a highly valuable channel as promoting my book on Amazon for people searching for, or browsing Marketing books has high intent. The drawback is that there is also a wide selection and a browsing mind set.

On AdWords, I planned a Gmail campaign which will show ads to people who receive newsletters from a select group of marketing publications and business ones. I also built a Display campaign, which will target in-market audiences looking to buy eBooks narrowed down by the keyword "Marketing;" this will hopefully show my ads to people with an intent to buy books and an interest in marketing.

For YouTube, I created an account on Famebit, an influencer marketplace which was purchased by Google and has a large selection of YouTuber's on it. In order to find the right influencers to create a video for the book. I will then promote it via AdWords as a video (YouTube) campaign.

These campaigns are relatively low cost. I am contemplating search campaigns and LinkedIn as well, for people looking specifically for digital marketing books and for marketers by title or groups. However, I may wait and see how my Display campaigns perform first, as Search while intent based may be too costly for an eBook's price point.

I also plan on promoting this book to bloggers from the industry not only with direct reach out but as a target audience with hopes of getting some PR. I will also use my blog to promote the book as well.

Naturally, like any marketing project, I will be testing various methods as well as working on my store fronts, keywords and other elements I can control and make adjustments as needed.

My Fellow Marketing Ninjas,

You have reached the end of this journey. This book was just a glimpse of what digital marketing is about. There are hundreds of other metrics, tools, and lessons to go over. I have tried to keep this book to the main important topics. And hopefully, I have given you enough of a taste for you to want to continue exploring and growing your digital marketing knowledge base.

Digital Marketing is an ever-evolving trade, and to stay ahead of the pack, you must build a strong base of knowledge and understanding, build real partnerships and expand your network every day. Try everything, take nothing at face value, and above all, enjoy each path, and embrace your journey. As a marketer, and one who advocates the importance of sharing, if you enjoyed this book, I would appreciate it if you would be my ambassador, spread the word, rate it on Amazon and help me reach my final marketing goal for this book, "Word of Mouth."

Special thanks to:

Mr. Nisso Moyal, who several years ago took a chance on a guy with no marketing background and helped him enter an exciting world full of challenges and opportunities.

Dr. Ruth Caplan-Moskovich and my wife, Alex Moskovich for their extensive help and support with editing, proofreading and bringing this book to life.

Ms. Lisa Dotson, for helping to cohesively structure the book.

Megan McCullough, for helping format the book.

Mrs. Dorit Rosenfeld, for always believing in me.

Made in the USA
Lexington, KY
28 January 2018